The Art of Tying the
Dry
Fly

Fly-Tying Illustrations by
Richard Bunse

Skip Morris

Frank Amato Publications
Portland, Oregon

DEDICATION

For reasons that haven't the slightest to do with fly tying, I dedicate this book to Selma and Olive.

ACKNOWLEDGEMENTS

My sincere thanks to the following fly tiers:

For detailed instructions for the tying of their patterns: René Harrop, Richard Bunse, Lee Clark, Craig Mathews, Rod Robbinson, and Jim Schollmeyer.

For sharing insight and experience: Dave Hughes, Rick Hafele, Randall Kaufmann, and John Hazel.

Finally, thanks to those who did such fine work with all the technical details and challenges that made *The Art of Tying the Dry Fly* possible: Brian Rose, Richard Bunse, Jim Schollmeyer, Tony Amato, Nick Amato, and Frank Amato.

Published in 1993 by Frank Amato Publications,
P.O. Box 82112, Portland, Oregon 97282

Softbound ISBN:1-878175-36-X
Hardbound ISBN:1-878175-37-8

All photographs taken by author except where noted.

Front and Back Cover Photographs: Brian Rose

Book Design: Tony Amato

Printed in Hong Kong

10 9 8 7 6 5 4 3 2

CONTENTS

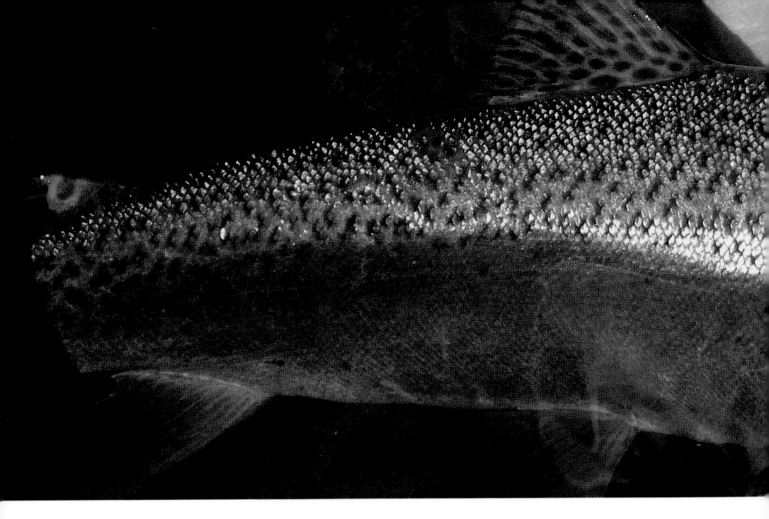

FOREWORD

There isn't much in fly fishing more exciting than catching fish on dry flies. Trout fishermen hold dry fly fishing as the pinnacle of the sport. Atlantic salmon and steelhead fishermen seem to feel the same way. They love to see the fish break the water's surface to take a fly.

Tying your own dry flies adds to this exciting aspect of fly fishing. In this book Skip Morris shares effective dry fly patterns, tying tricks and techniques that will improve the dry flies you will tie.

The book contains a wonderful cross section of standard trout patterns as well as new fly tying innovations. Dry fly patterns for mayflies, caddis, stoneflies and terrestrials are included.

I know that Skip understands all aspects of fly tying skills. How do I know? Each issue of *Flyfishing* Magazine features flies tied by Skip on the cover or contents page. These are the flies from the "Fly Wrap Up" section. They include everything from delicate, tiny mayflies to outrageous, packed deer hair bass bugs. Each fly he provides for the magazine is an example of perfection.

Skip brings his 30 years of dry fly tying experience to the assistance of the tier in this volume. Skip often exhibits his fly tying talent at various sportsman's shows and fishing clubs. Many of Skip's flies have found their way into the Cushner Fly Museum in Florence, Oregon. Skip's mounted flies are actively sought by collectors.

Here then, is a book that will provide you with a wealth of information and instruction on tying better dry flies.

-Marty Sherman, Editor, *Flyfishing* Magazine
February 3, 1993
Portland, Oregon

INTRODUCTION

Despite the fact that no book on the dry fly can ever be complete, this one contains the best of what I've learned after tying dry flies for over 30 years. Here are long-established flies and others from fresh new perspectives, flies of complex construction and others of utter simplicity—what they have in common is that all are practical; all can take trout with deadly efficiency.

I say "can" because the effectiveness of any fly depends on both how it is fished and how appropriate it is to the moment. And though this is a fly-tying book, there is information here to help you fish these flies appropriately and effectively.

There are choices here too, but all fly fishers like choices. Choices provide us room to experiment, room to play, and that's part of the fun. So you can try the Jay-Dave's Hopper and the Letort Hopper, the Thorax Dun and the Bunse Dun, the Grizzly Wulff and the Rat-Faced McDougal and decide what flies you like, where you like to fish them, and when.

I've been fortunate. I've been able to draw from books and articles, videos, and the openness of many exceptional tiers. Certainly, novice tiers have instructed me as well—who better to illuminate the essential and recurring difficulties of fly tying and to serve as models for the testing of solutions? I've been blessed with the opportunity to share what they've given me, along with my own discoveries, at sportsman's shows, lectures, clinics, and through private instruction, articles and books. In turn, the teaching of fly tying has been an opportunity to rehearse and pare down information to its clearest, most useful form. For all this I've been fortunate indeed. May my good fortune, through this book, be yours.

So let *The Art of Tying the Dry Fly* be a guide to technique, a source for useful fly patterns, a tool for creativity, and a source of fascination and pleasure. In every word I've spoken or written about fly tying, it is my hope that I've given something of value to fly fishers—and *that* can never equal what fly fishers and fly fishing have given me. Here, you are welcome to much more than one tier's experience with dry flies; you are also welcome to the best of what so many have given freely.

- Skip Morris, July 7, 1992

COMPONENTS OF THE DRY FLY

Classic Dry Fly

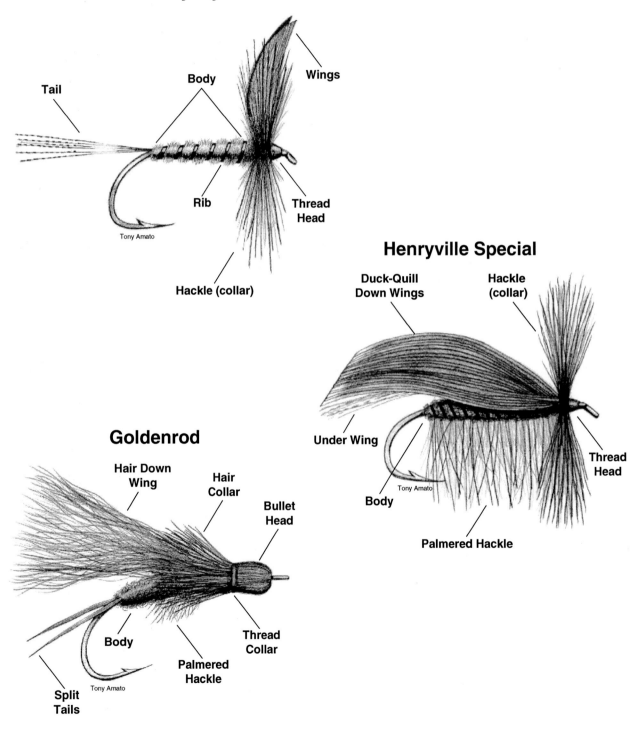

Tail

Body

Wings

Rib

Thread
Head

Tony Amato

Hackle (collar)

Henryville Special

Duck-Quill
Down Wings

Hackle
(collar)

Under Wing

Body

Tony Amato

Thread
Head

Palmered Hackle

Goldenrod

Hair Down
Wing

Hair
Collar

Bullet
Head

Body

Palmered
Hackle

Thread
Collar

Tony Amato

Split
Tails

I
ESSENTIAL TECHNIQUES

"Essential" is the word—these techniques you will use constantly. They are listed alphabetically for quick reference. Tying instructions for specific flies will refer to these techniques as they are called for. Section X, "Basic Techniques," describes other more-specialized techniques.

Adding Head Cement

All you need do is dip the tip of something pointed—a hat pin, bodkin, round toothpick—into a thin head cement and work the cement quickly around the fly's thread head. The thin cement will soak into the thread and dry rapidly, but you must watch that you add enough cement to secure the thread head without adding so much that it floods into and stiffens the fly's soft materials or fills the hook's eye. Epoxy glue, my favorite head cement (see section XIII, "Dry-Fly Tools"), is fairly thick, so a tiny amount is added to the head and teased out into an even layer followed by more epoxy until the head is neatly covered. But for heaven's sake, keep the epoxy out of the hook's eye—epoxy is tough to remove. Flies freshly coated with any head cement can be stuck into wood or foam blocks until the coatings harden.

1. Coating a thread head with epoxy.

Dubbing

The word "dubbing" has two meanings to the fly tier: It is fur or synthetic fibers spun onto thread, and it is the action of adding fur or synthetic fibers to a fly. So tiers routinely use dubbing when dubbing their flies.

For right handers, cradle the bobbin in the palm of your left hand and clutch it lightly with your second, third, and fourth fingers; hold a ball of dubbing between your left-hand

thumb and finger. There should be a few inches of bare thread between the fly and the tip of the bobbin's tube. Waxing the thread helps dubbing, but it's not required; another good approach is to rub the wax on your fingertip instead of on the thread. At any rate, now is the time to add wax if you so choose. With your right-hand thumb and first finger, draw a tiny amount of dubbing from the side of the dubbing ball; drawing the dubbing this way tends to align the fibers, which makes for the toughest dubbed flies. Use very little dubbing, as almost all beginning fly tiers use far too much. In fact, the best way is to start with almost no dubbing, and then add more until you have the right amount—which won't take much.

Hold the dubbing to the bare thread as close as you comfortably can to the hook; most of the fibers should be at a right angle to the thread. Spin the dubbing and thread between your right-hand thumb and first finger; spin in one direction only, otherwise you are spinning the dubbing on and then off.

Slide the dubbing up to the hook (or simply take a few extra thread turns later to start the dubbing onto the hook). Continue adding dubbing in this manner until all you need is on the thread, but cover no more than four inches of thread with dubbing—more than four inches requires too large an orbit with your bobbin which in turn makes for slow tying, so add more dubbing to the thread after the four inches is on the hook. Once the dubbing is on the thread, all that remains is to wrap it tightly up the shank.

A few pointers. Dubbing, unlike most materials that are wrapped around a hook, can be neatly backed over itself to build diameter or fill in gaps. Tapered dubbed bodies can be created by adding the dubbing to the thread from almost none near the hook to thicker near the bobbin, or a tapered body can be created by building the dubbing layer by layer. For tiny flies, add dubbing to the thread in amounts so small that you can hardly see it—it will show up just fine once it is spun on.

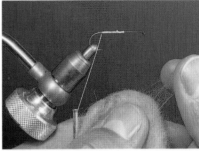

1. Hold a ball of dubbing in one hand and draw fibers from the ball's edge with your other hand.

2. Hold the dubbing against the thread.

3. Spin the dubbing and thread between your thumb and finger in *one* direction only.

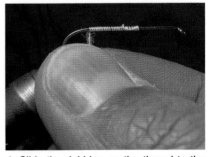

4. Slide the dubbing up the thread to the hook. Continue adding dubbing to the thread.

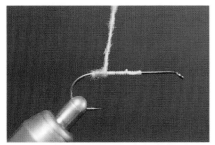

5. Wrap the dubbing-layered thread up the shank.

This is the basic method for dubbing; other alternate methods are described in section X, "Basic Techniques" under "Dubbing."

The Half Hitch

The half hitch is a simple fly tier's knot sometimes used in place of the more-involved whip finish to secure a thread head; three half hitches are usually used for this. When the half hitch becomes routine, it is time to tackle the whip finish. But there are other uses for the half hitch which, if you haven't already, you'll discover. Here is how it's performed (right-handers):

Begin with the thread coming from the rear of the head. Release enough thread so that there is about 7 inches between the bobbin and the hook. Hold the bobbin in your left hand and bring it up toward you until it is level with the hook; only light tension need be applied to the thread. Extend the first and second fingers of your right hand and separate them about 1 inch. Bring the tips of your spread right-hand fingers down onto the thread; the palm of your right hand should be down. Now rotate and drop the wrist of your right hand until your right-hand's two fingers point up; as you do this, raise the bobbin, and then bring it down to the left until it is again level with the hook and the thread crosses itself in an "X."

At this point, the right-hand fingers should be pointing up and should be inside a loop of thread; the left hand, and the bobbin, should be to the left and level with the hook. In essence, you have already formed the half hitch; all that remains is to get it onto the fly's head and tightened.

Hook one side of the half-hitch loop over the fly's head. Hold the loop over the fly and then catch the loop with the first finger of the left hand; it is easiest to catch the loop *between* the two right-hand fingers.

Slip your right hand-fingers out of the loop; with your right hand, pick up something to guide the loop as it closes: scissors, a needle, bodkin, or hat pin. Use this object to take the loop from the left-hand finger. Draw the bobbin down or toward you with your left hand as you guide the loop closed with the object in your right.

1. Create a half-hitch loop and hook it over the thread head.

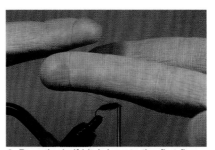

2. Pass the half-hitch loop to the first finger on your left hand.

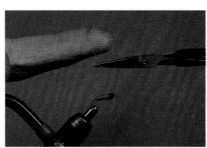

3. Take the loop from the finger with a hat-pin, bodkin, or your scissors' tip.

4. Guide the loop closed.

Half hitch

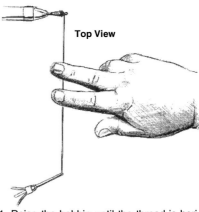

Top View

1. Raise the bobbin until the thread is horizontal. Spread your first and second fingers and bring them down until tips lay on thread.

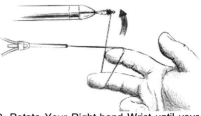

2. Rotate Your Right-hand Wrist until your fingers and palm point up; as you do this, raise the bobbin and then lower it to the left. The thread should cross over itself in an"X".

3. Hook the far side of the loop over the head.

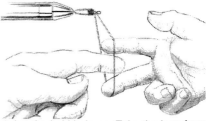

4. Let the bobbin hang. Take the loop from your right-hand fingers with the first finger of your left hand.

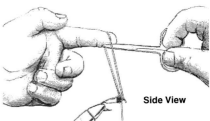

Side View

5. Insert scissors a bodkin, or hatpin into the loop with your right-hand and remove your left-hand finger.

6. Pull on the bobbin as you guide the half-hitch loop closed.

The Light Turn

The light-tension thread turn, which I simply call the "light turn," is a handy, quicker alternative to the pinch for tying in stiffer materials such as wire and hackle stems. As an example, I'll describe how to use a light turn to tie in some oval gold tinsel.

Hold the tinsel near its end (oval tinsel is about as soft a material as you can comfortably tie in with a light turn). Hold the end of the tinsel along the shank at the tie-in point. If you hold the tinsel's end slightly towards your side of the shank, the thread's torque will draw the tinsel up on top of the shank. Bring the thread up and over the tinsel's end and down the far side, and then pull the thread tight. Add a few more tight turns of thread before proceeding.

The trick to making a good light turn is to use very light thread tension—just enough to control the thread but not so much that the material is forced to slide around ahead of the thread.

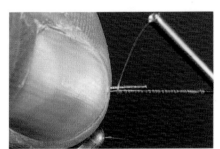

1. The light turn requires light thread tension.

The Pinch

The pinch is a technique used for tying in soft materials; it also offers excellent control. Here is how to execute it:

Hold the material between your left-hand thumb and first finger at the tie-in point on the hook's shank (right-hander's instructions). Bring your bobbin toward you and then straight up over the hook while main-taining constant, firm thread tension. Move your left hand back slightly, but instead of sliding the thumb and finger back, *roll* their tips as you draw their joints closer together—this will widen the space at the front of the tips. Move the bobbin rearwards, towards the hook's bend, bringing the thread back between your thumb's tip and the material; keep bringing the thread back until it nestles securely in this spot.

With only slight tension on the thread, bring the bobbin back and down the far side of the hook as you guide the thread in between your fingertip and the material. You now have a loop of thread around the material. Move your left hand slightly forward and widen the space between your thumb and finger joints—your thumb and finger tips should now hold the material securely and enclose the loop of thread. Pull the thread tight, in turn closing the loop. Note that you have tied in a soft material while controlling its position on the hook.

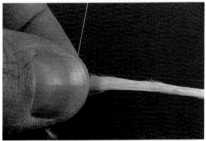

Performing the pinch.

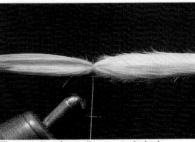

The results of a well-executed pinch.

The Pinch

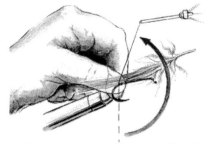

1. Hold the material to the shank. Raise the bobbin.

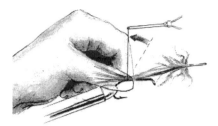

2. Bring the joints of your thumb and finger closer together; this will spread apart your thumbtip from your fingertip; slip the thread back between thumbtip and material.

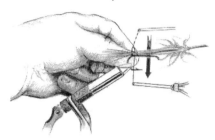

3. Bring the thread (and bobbin) down the far side of the material as you draw the thread back between fingertip and material.

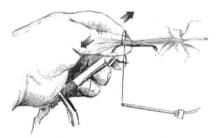

4. Widen the gap between your thumb and finger joint closing thumbtip and fingertip around the loop.

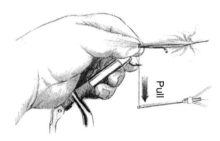

5. Pull down on the bobbin, tighten the pinch loop.

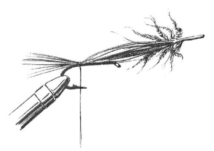

6. The material should be secured atop the hook.

Starting Thread

To start thread on a hook's shank, simply make four tight thread turns forward (toward the hook's eye), and then five or six tight turns back over the first four. Cut or break the thread's end and start tying.

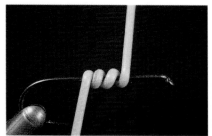

1. Make four thread turns forward (fly line is used for clarity).

2. Make six turns back to lock the thread onto the shank.

The Triangle

The "triangle" is my name for a method of forcing materials back from a hook's eye for ease in building a thread head. The name comes from the shape of the tiny opening formed when the thumb's tip and the tips of the first and second fingers are brought together.

To execute the triangle, simply slip this opening over the hook's eye and allow just enough slack to let the thread slip through. Then draw your thumb and fingers' tips back pulling hackle fibers, dubbing, or whatever material is near the eye back for clear tying access. On tiny flies you will be able to use only your thumb and one finger, but the motion is essentially the same.

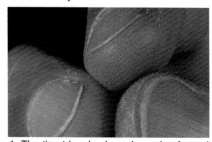

1. The tiny triangle-shaped opening formed by the thumb and fingers' tips

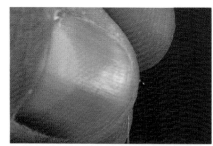

2. Draw the opening back over the eye.

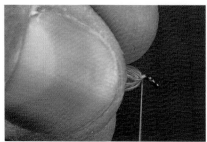

3. Draw back the thumb and fingers' tips, letting the thread slip past, and clearing the area behind the hook's eye.

The Thread Head

The thread head is merely thread wraps that cover material ends and build to a tapered shape. Sometimes, especially with heads that are large, steeply tapered, or both, it helps to add very tight thread turns near the eye, and then diminish the thread's tension as the thread travels up the head—the wraps at the eye form a solid foundation to keep the lighter turns from slipping (although all the wraps should be at least snug).

Leaving plenty of space behind the eye helps avoid steep heads and the awkwardness of too little head space. The trend is towards tiny fly heads. I like a small head, but this is really a matter of style and personal preference.

1. Two thread heads: one is neat and tiny; the other is large but clean and gradually tapered.

The Whip Finish

The whip finish has intimidated more than one fly tier, which is a shame, because the whip finish is really only a half hitch that forgot to stop—it's easy. Look at it this way: The half hitch is a loop in which one of its sides is wrapped around the other; the whip finish is created when the side of the loop doing the wrapping adds more than one wrap.

Begin by adding a half hitch at the rear of the thread-head, but stop as soon as the half-hitch loop is hooked over the head. At this point, you have the side of the loop that is doing the wrapping, which we will call the "working" side, and the side of the loop which is being wrapped over, which we will call the "passive" side. The working side will be nearest you, and the passive side will be farthest from you. Grasp the working side in your left hand and hold it straight up under tension; then remove your right-hand fingers from the loop. As long as tension is maintained on the working side, it should keep the passive side firmly locked in place.

Now all you need to do is maintain tension on the working side as you pass it from hand to hand and wrap it towards the eye in three turns; as you do this, keep the passive side out in front of the fly—don't let the passive side slip behind the working side, or the turns you are adding will fail to enhance the whip finish's security. Close the whip-finish loop as you would a half-hitch loop, trim the thread, and add head cement.

1. Start the whip finish as you would a half-hitch; slip the loop over the thread head.

2. Lift up firmly on the working side of the loop and release the passive side.

3. Pass the working side from hand to hand as you add three turns over the passive side.

4. Close the loop as usual.

The Whip Finish

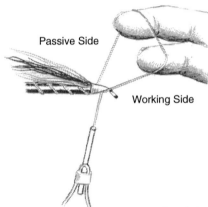

Passive Side

Working Side

1. Proceed as you would for a half hitch by slipping the loop over the head.

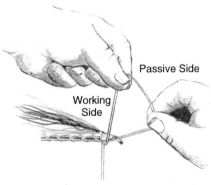

Passive Side

Working Side

2. Let the bobbin hang. Bring the passive side of the loop forward and keep it there as you wrap the working side forward in three turns.

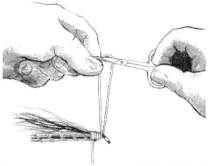

3. Insert scissors (or another pointed object) into the loop and take the loop from your left hand.

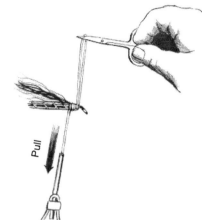

Pull

4. Pull the bobbin down as you guide the loop closed.

II

MAYFLY IMITATIONS

Introduction To Mayflies

One has only to explore the writings of such historic angling figures as Flick, Fox, and Halford to see that the mayfly has long been the model for dry-fly design. While the importance of other trout-stream insects has finally been recognized, the mayfly is still as significant as any.

Mayflies range from the tiny *Tricorythodes*, merely a white speck at a rod's distance, to the massive lake fly *Hexagenia* that emerges bright yellow at twilight. Various species of mayflies live in water ranging from the stillness of lakes to the quick, broken water of current-loving stoneflies. Because there are so many variations in mayfly color, size, and habitat, the most useful fly dressings for mayflies are flexible—the materials stay the same regardless of color or size. But water type is often a factor in selecting a fly pattern; Al troth's Dark Green Drake, for example, is designed to stay afloat on exactly the kind of lively water from which the natural green drake emerges.

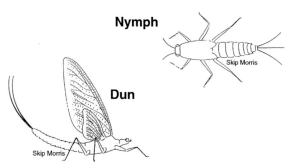

Nymph

Skip Morris

Dun

Skip Morris

There are three stages in the life cycle of a mayfly: the "nymph," the immature form that dominates most of the mayfly's life span; the "dun," the adult that has escaped its shuck and unfurled its graceful wings at the water's surface; and the "spinner," the final, brief form that concentrates on mating and releasing its fertilized eggs until it has accomplished both and then quickly weakens and dies.

There is some variation in mayfly hatching, but most species swim to the surface in open water to hatch.

This and their long wing-drying rest atop the surface make their survival around trout tenuous. Again the mayfly is easy prey when the females follow their egg laying by falling helpless and dying to the surface. It is generally the dun and spinner stages that concern the dry-fly tier, although the half nymph-half dun condition of a partially hatched mayfly is receiving increased interest from anglers and tiers—it appears that the trout have been interested in it all along.

Identifying the mayfly dun is easy—of the common stream and lake insects, only the mayfly holds its wings upright as though it were a tiny sailboat.

Section V on traditional dry flies presents flies that were once the standard choice for imitating mayflies. Traditional dry flies are still good for this and for general-purpose dry-fly fishing, but the trend over the last twenty-or-so years has been towards flies that more precisely resemble the outline and posture of the natural.

So how do you choose between Comparaduns, parachutes, and other mayfly patterns? You can begin by considering water type—a well-hackled parachute fly will stay afloat on rougher water than Thorax Duns can handle. If a bushy parachute fly fails to stay up, it is time to turn to the "Rough-Water Flies" section. Beyond this, most anglers try what's around, and then make flexible choices; that's a sound precept.

TYING DIFFICULTY
1 is easy; 5 is difficult

Poly Wing Spinner	2
Thorax Dun	3
Comparadun	3
Dark Green Drake	4
Paradrake	5
Bunse Dun	5

The Poly Wing Spinner and CDC-Wing Spinner

This is about as easy to tie as a fly gets. I have never been able to determine who created the Poly Wing Spinner, but I suspect that once someone suggested the idea of a spinner pattern with a poly-yarn wing, the rest was obvious. The Speckled Poly Wing Spinner shown here is only a sample; you can and should vary the size and colors of this fly to imitate all sorts of mayfly spinners.

The crinkly yarn suggests the fluting in a mayfly's wing. This particular version of the Poly Wing Spinner imitates the "speckled spinner," a slow-water and lake mayfly found all across America, though the speckled spinner's greatest importance seems to be in the western states. This mayfly passes through several generations in a single season, each smaller than the last, hence the wide range of hook sizes. Normally it is best to fish a Poly Wing Spinner dead drift to rising trout; with the Speckled Poly Wing Spinner, however, I often give it just the tiniest quiver to catch the trout's eye.

SPECKLED POLY WING SPINNER

HOOK: Standard dry fly, sizes 18 to 12 (the hook shown is an Eagle Claw D59F).
THREAD: Gray 8/0 or 6/0.
TAIL: Medium-blue-dun hackle fibers, split.
ABDOMEN: Medium-gray dubbing (shown is muskrat fur).
WINGS: Gray poly yarn.
THORAX: Medium-gray dubbing (shown is muskrat fur).

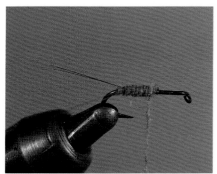

1. Tie in the split tails (any of the three methods described in section X, "Basic Techniques" under "Split Tails"); then dub a tapered body up two-thirds of the shank.

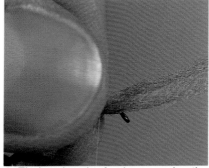

2. Tie in a bunch of poly yarn using the pinch, and then add a second tight turn of thread.

3. Pull the yarn's tips out to the sides of the hook and crisscross the yarn at its tie-in point with turns of thread.

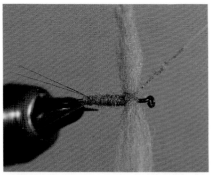

4. Dub around the yarn's tie-in point with crisscrossed turns. Dub forward to just behind the eye, and complete a thread head as usual.

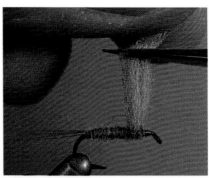

5. Draw up the wings and cut them to length with a single snip.

6. To tie the Harrop CDC spinner wing, start the fly by measuring and then tying in two CDC feathers about three-quarters up the shank using the wing pinch. Add the tail and abdomen, and then set the wings just as you would set wood-duck wings—but stop after the crisscrossed thread turns have spread the wings to the sides.

7. Over the top of the wings, use crisscrossed thread wraps to tie in a section of Z-lon. Complete the fly as usual and then trim the Z-lon. (See the pattern for a Harrop spinner imitation, the CDC Rusty Spinner, in section XVII, "Additional Dry Flies.")

The Thorax Dun

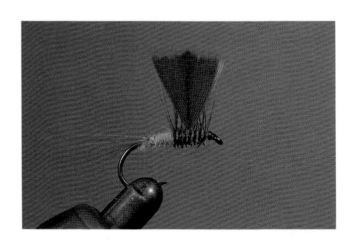

Vincent Marinaro, author of the revolutionary *Modern Dry Fly Code*, deserves credit for developing the thorax-style dry fly, but the fly we will explore here is different than Marinaro's. His original thorax fly was of radical design and a bit awkward to tie; the thorax fly shown here evolved slowly over the years and seems to be the choice of both tiers and anglers.

Turkey flats—broad, stout feathers with straight-edged tips—are used for the wings of most thorax flies, but almost any flat feather will do—pheasant, hen saddle, partridge, mallard, duck shoulder—which is fortunate, because turkey flats are expensive and a lot of waste results from using only the very tips of two of these large feathers for a single fly. Another common wing for Thorax Duns is the "bunched" wing, simply a single upright clump of fibers.

The Hendrickson Thorax imitates the important eastern hendrickson mayfly. But the thorax style is used to imitate many different mayflies simply by varying colors.

HENDRICKSON THORAX

HOOK: Standard dry fly, sizes 14 and 12 (the hook shown is a Dai-Riki model 305).
THREAD: Gray 8/0 or 6/0.
WINGS: Medium-gray turkey flats or substitute.
TAIL: Medium-dun hackle fibers, split.
BODY: Pale-pink dubbing (poly dubbing, dyed rabbit, or as with the classic imitation, urine-burned fox).
HACKLE: Medium blue dun.

1. Pair, measure, and tie in the wings about two-thirds up the shank from the bend using the pinch.

2. Tie in the split tails (the first method from section X, "Basic Techniques"is shown).

3. Dub a tapered body to the center of the shank. Raise the wings, crease them upright with your thumb nail, support their position with tight thread turns against their front, and then tie in the hackle at midshank.

4. Dub to just behind the eye, spiral the hackle forward in five to seven turns, roughly half the turns behind the wing and half in front. Tie off the hackle, trim its tip closely, build a small thread head, add a whip finish, trim the thread, add head cement. (You can add the head cement after the next step if you prefer.)

5. Trim the underside of the hackle flat so that the hackle forms a fan or half-circle on the top half of the fly.

Duck Wings

Duck shoulder feathers should be found in the circled areas.

6. A properly trimmed hackle.

Alternate Wing Tie In Method
(Duck shoulder and others)

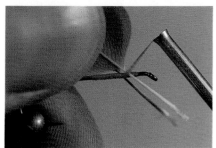

7. Some wing feathers, such as the duck-shoulder feather shown, roll out of position with the standard wing pinch. So instead, hold the stripped stems of the feathers down both sides of the hook and secure the stems with light-tension thread turns; the first turns, as shown, go across the front of the stems atop the hook to behind the stems below. (Floss is substituted for thread to help illustrate.)

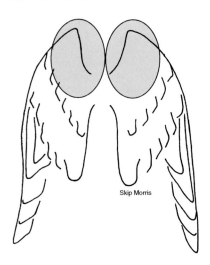

Skip Morris

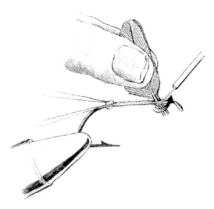

1. With the stems down both sides of the shank, take a couple of light-tension thread turns from the front of the stems atop the hook to the rear of the stems below.

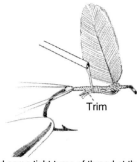

2. Take two light-tension thread turns the other way—from the rear of the stems atop the shank to the front of the stems below.

3. Add some tight turns of thread at the previous angles to really secure the wings, and then draw back the stems; secure them with thread turns and trim them.

Trim

8. Take a couple of light-tension turns the opposite way—across the rear of the stems atop the hook and across their front below.

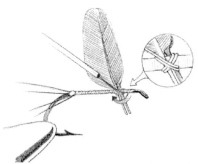

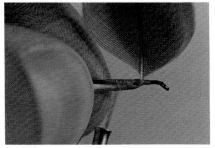

9. Add a few tight thread turns from both angles; then bend the stems back along the shank, bind and trim them. With this method of tying in the wings, it is best to tie in the split tails first, tie in the wings, tie in the hackle, and then return to the bend and dub forward to just short of the eye.

10. Alternate wings: grizzly hen neck, and duck shoulder.

The Comparadun And The Sparkle Dun

If the Comparadun is not the most popular style of dry fly in America at this writing, I'd be surprised. This fly has been steadily growing in popularity since it was first revealed in 1972 by Al Caucci and Bob Nastasi through their book *Comparahatch*.

What makes the Comparadun significantly different from other flies is its fan-shaped wing of deer hair. The best hair I have found for this wing is coastal deer hair; most fly shops carry it.

The Comparadun Quill Gordon imitates the eastern quill-gordon mayfly. It hatches as early as April, emerging in the afternoon from quick water. More than just another productive mayfly hatch, the emergence of the quill gordon signals the beginning of dry-fly fishing to many eastern fly fishers; faith in the quill gordon hatch sends anglers out to wade and cast in chill, rain, and even snow.

The Comparadun wing deserves a few pointers regarding its construction. First there is the matter of getting the hair wing firmly mounted; you may want to start with 3/0 thread so that you can really bear down, or use 3/0 throughout. Richard Bunse wraps thread from the wing's butts to the shank and back repeatedly, using the shank wraps as an anchor. Another problem is distributing the hair evenly; sometimes this wing ends up heavy at its top and sparse at its edges. The best wing is even throughout. Here is one solution: Work the wing hairs slightly down the sides of the hook as you tie in the wing (rocking the wing as you work it down can help). Beyond this, be aggressive in setting the wing upright—press it up sharply with your thumbnail and secure the position with plenty of tight turns of thread firmly up against the wing's base.

The Sparkle Dun is shown at the end of the tying-sequence photographs. It is a variation of the Comparadun and was created by Craig Mathews of Blue Ribbon Flies. The Sparkle Dun is tied in exactly the same manner as the Comparadun with the exception of the tail—a shank-length tuft of sparkle yarn is the Sparkle Dun's tail. The tuft suggests the partially discarded shuck of a hatching mayfly. I've fished the Sparkle Dun to great effect; try it.

COMPARADUN QUILL GORDON

HOOK: Standard dry fly, sizes 14 and 12 (the hook shown is a Partridge GRS3A).
THREAD: Olive (or gray) 8/0 or 6/0 (you can also start with 3/0, and switch, or simply continue with 3/0).
WING: Coastal deer hair of medium hue.
TAIL: Two to four dark-gray Micro Fibetts (or hackle fibers, especially on sizes 16 and under), split; olive brown Z-lon or sparkle poly yarn for the Sparkle Dun's shuck.
BODY: Light-gray dubbing with a dash of yellow (Caucci and Nastasi prefer rabbit fur dubbing for all Comparaduns).

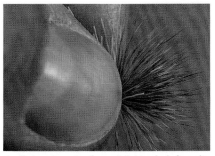

1. Snip a bunch of coastal deer hair from its hide; comb, measure (from eye to midbend as usual), and tie in the hair about one-quarter of the shank's length back from the eye using the pinch. Stack the hair if you wish, but coastal deer is usually well-stacked on the hide; careful handling will keep it that way.

2. Still holding the wing butts after the pinch, raise them and snip them at an angle. Cover the trimmed butts with thread. If you are using 3/0 thread, you now have the option of switching to 8/0 or 6/0.

3. Tie in the split tails. (My thread-ball-and-trim method won't work with Micro Fibetts, so use one of the other two methods if Micro Fibetts are used.)

4. Dub a tapered body to the rear of the wing. Set the wing upright by slipping your thumbnail under it (and over the eye) and right up against the base of the wing; then rotate your thumbnail up and back to really crease the wing's base. Repeat this once on each side of the wing using either your thumbnail or fingernail.

5. Draw the wing firmly back and add tight turns of bare thread right at its base for support.

6. (Bottom view.) Crisscross dubbed thread from the front of the wing to the back and again to the front a few times to cover the underside of the wing; then dub to just behind the eye and complete the thread head as usual.

7. The Comparadun wing: front view.

8. The same fly tied in Sparkle Dun style—a shuck of Z-lon or sparkle poly yarn replaces the split tails.

The Dark Green Drake

Fly tier, fly designer, guide Al Troth has given us many innovative, productive fly patterns; here is one well worth exploring. The Dark Green Drake imitates a western mayfly called the green drake, an insect that inspires lots of trout, including some huge ones, to feed on the surface. Spring and summer are green-drake time. The duns struggle and tumble back in their efforts to take flight—trout take full advantage of this.

The eastern green drake is an entirely different species than the western, but it is also big, even slightly bigger than the western, and it can also be imitated well with a parachute pattern. The colors of the eastern green drake—creamy yellow body with brown ribs, light-gray wings, molted cream-brown legs—incorporated into the Mike Lawson Paradrake or Al Troth's Dark Green Drake shown here result in a good imitation.

The parachute hackle and overall style of this dressing can be used to imitate many other mayfly species; vary the colors, hook size, and even the materials as you need or desire. I have included some substitute materials—Al's original choices are best, but some of his materials may require some hunting, and the substitutes work.

Some tiers have trouble creating a parachute-style hackle, but a few simple pointers will make the task flow—see "Parachute Hackles" in section XI, "Hackle—Still The Standard."

DARK GREEN DRAKE

HOOK: Standard dry fly or 1X or 2X long, sizes 12 to 10 depending on shank length (longer shank, smaller size). (The hook shown is a Tiemco 5212.)
THREAD: Green or olive 8/0 or 6/0.
WING: Clump of black poly yarn.
HACKLE: Grizzly dyed insect green (insect green is a bright, yellowish green; I often substitute brown).
TAIL: Black elk hair (I often substitute moose-body hair).
RIB: Yellow embroidery yarn (I sometimes substitute single-strand floss).
BODY: Olive dubbing (Al prefers olive poly dubbing and olive dyed hare's mask fur in a 50-50 mix; I use just the poly dubbing).

1. Start the thread, and then, using the pinch, tie in the poly yarn securely. Trim the butts of the poly yarn at an angle and bind them with thread turns. Add a few thread turns around the base of the yarn (not around the shank), and then draw back the thread firmly to set the wing upright. Secure the thread in a few tight turns.

2. Wrap the thread lightly up and down the base of the wing. Secure the hackle by its stem to this wing base by running the thread again up and down the wing base, but this time use more thread tension. Draw the hackle's stem back along the shank and secure it with thread turns. Trim the stem. (See "Parachute Hackles" in section XI, "Hackle—Still The Standard.")

3. Comb and stack a bunch of tail hair. Tie in the hair tail using the pinch. Trim the butts of the tail at an angle so the hair butts lap the wing butts.

4. Tie in the rib and then dub a tapered body up to the rear of the wing.

5. Wrap the rib up the dubbed body in several evenly spaced turns. Tie off and trim the rib. Add more dubbing behind the wing base and in front of it until the bare thread ends up about 1/16" behind the hook's eye.

6. Wind the hackle down the wing base in tight, consecutive turns to the body. Let the hackle pliers hang on the far side of the hook as you draw the hackle fibers back and secure the hackle's tip with thread turns. Release the fibers and trim the hackle's tip closely.

7. Draw back the hackle fibers again and build a tapered thread head. Release the fibers and slip a whip finish over the thread head, and then trim the thread. Remove the fly from the vise and trim its wing to shape with scissors. Add head cement (add a drop of head cement at the top of the hackle against the wing base for added durability if you like).

8. Another wing method. Tie in a section of poly yarn as you would for spent spinner wings (see "The Poly Wing Spinner and CDC-Wing Spinner"). Rotate the yarn to the underside of the shank.

9. Draw the ends of the yarn up firmly and work a couple of tight thread turns around the yarn atop the shank. Crisscross tight thread turns underneath the hump of yarn beneath the shank to really secure the wing. Proceed with step 2 and on.

The Paradrake

The first fly I saw called a "Paradrake" was the Swisher-Richards pattern designed to imitate big mayflies such as the western gray drake and both the eastern and western green drakes. The Paradrake described here was made popular by Mike Lawson; it and similar variations are the Paradrakes you will see most often in catalogs and along trout rivers.

Here are a few pointers for tying the Paradrake: When you fold back the elk hair to form the body, start by pushing your finger straight into the hair, in line with the shank, to flare the hair away from the eye. Then pull the hair to both sides of the hook, and back around both sides of the wing. Finally, as you draw it back for the forming of the body, stroke the hair a time or two to even the tension throughout the hairs. When you reach the hair extension with the thread, hold the tips of the hair in one hand (the left hand for right-handers and vise versa) and work the thread with the other; pass the bobbin behind the vise each time, and

then hold the thread with the little finger of the hand holding the hair extension, and pull each thread turn snug (not tight) before adding the next.

The Brown Drake Paradrake imitates the big brown drake, which is distributed across America. Brown Drakes prefer lazy currents and still waters and hatch at twilight from May through July with peak activity usually occurring sometime in the first two weeks of June.

BROWN DRAKE PARADRAKE

HOOK: Standard dry fly, size 12 and 10 (the hook shown is a Gamakatsu F 13).
THREAD: Black 3/0.
TAIL: Natural dark moose body.
WING: Natural tan elk hair.
BODY: Natural tan-brown elk hair (leader core optional).
HACKLE: Grizzly dyed yellow (as this is an unusual hackle, you can substitute a regular grizzly or light-brown hackle) one size larger than normal (size-12 hook takes size- 10 hackle).

  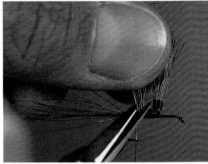

1. Tie some leader in at midshank and spiral the thread down it to the bend (optional). Comb, stack, and measure a small bunch of elk hair and then tie it in, using the pinch, at midshank as a wing; the hair should extend from its tie-in point about twice the length of the hook's shank. Trim the hairs' butts at an angle and thread bind them.

2. Set the wing upright with thread (see "The Parachute Hackle" in section XI, "Hackle—Still the Standard"), and then wrap a layer of thread up, and then another back down its base.

3. Comb, stack, and tie in about ten moose-body hairs as a tail. The tail should extend from the bend about two shank lengths. Trim the tail's butts at an angle over the wing butts. Thread bind the tail's butts.

4. Comb a bunch of elk hair, and then work its butts around the eye and shank and tie it in as shown. Secure it with plenty of tight thread turns just behind the eye, and then trim and thread bind the hair's butts.

5. Draw the hair back along both sides of the shank and around the wing. Make a few tight thread turns right in front of the wing; this will create a sort of head-thorax.

6. Spiral the thread tightly down the deer hair to the end of the shank.

7. Continue spiralling the thread down the elk hair a distance of about half to three-quarters the length of the shank. At this point, add a few tight thread turns. Reversing the hook in your vise can make this task easy. (If you want the extension to tip up, tip it well up as you thread wrap it.

8. Spiral the thread back to the wing base. (If you reversed the hook, switch it in the vise again after the thread reaches the beginning of the hair extension, that is, after it reaches the hook.)

9. Tie the hackle in along the thread wraps at the base of the wing with one layer of thread up the base and stem and then another back down. Secure the hackle's stem with a couple of tight thread turns at the thread collar ahead of the wings, and then trim the stem closely.

10. Wrap the hackle down the wing base in consecutive turns. Let the hackle pliers hang on the far side of the hook. Draw the hackle fibers up and back; tie off and trim the hackle's tip. Whip finish the thread collar.

11. Trim away the leader and all but three of the stacked elk-hair fibers at the rear of the extended body. Add head cement to the rear of the body, to the top of the hackle at the wing's base, and to the thread collar in front of the wing.

The Bunse Dun

By the time I had fished one, I had heard and read a lot about the Bunse Dun. I had even seen Richard Bunse tie one at the annual Oregon Federation of Fly Fishers' Fly Tying Exposition.

We were both demonstrating there, and that was where I first met Richard.

A year later, Richard offered to take me and a cameraman on a float trip for a local television show of which I am host. That day, Richard brought the flies, and I got some experience with the Bunse Dun. A day of fishing Bunse Duns should convince anyone that they are worth the time it takes to tie them.

It does take a while to tie a Bunse Dun, even for Richard, and the first few you tie may be unacceptable; but once you get the hang of tying it, and see how well it floats, endures, and deceives trout, you will consider tying the Bunse Dun time well spent. But I want to be honest—this fly is tricky to tie.

The Bunse Dun is durable, buoyant, and exceptionally lifelike. By varying its sizes and colors it can imitate a variety of mayfly species. The body material is called "ethafoam," a foam sheeting that is used mostly for packing. Richard discovered it when he found it wrapped around the frames he uses for his artwork. Ethafoam is often found wrapped around such things as fine electronics, camera lenses, picture frames and, in the thickest sheeting, appliances. You'll have to hunt it down for now (though a single find will last a long time, and there is lots of it out there), but I hope that some fly-tying materials supply will see the light and offer ethafoam soon. The finest sheeting is about 3/64" thick and is used for hook sizes 18 and 20, the 1/16" thick sheeting is for hook sizes 16 and 14, and the thickest sheeting, about 3/32" thick, is for Bunse Duns on hooks size 12 and larger.

A few guidelines are in order. The dimensions of the cut sheeting will have a lot to do with tying ease—too wide a pattern makes a bulging thorax, and too thin a pattern will make a skimpy thorax that won't reach over the top of the shank. The extension on a Bunse Dun is normally four sections, but you can add a section for the largest flies and eliminate one for the smallest—if this doesn't make sense now, it will soon. When sliding the body off the needle, I like to get my thumbnail and fingernail right down against the needle behind the foam—this seems to eliminate the danger of having the inner thread turns slip out of the body. The tightness of the thread turns around the thorax will largely determine its bulk. Regarding all these points: practice, experiment.

The Bunse Dun shown imitates the mayflies *Rhithrogena morrisoni* and *Rhithrogena hageni*, commonly called march browns. It was the march-brown hatch we fished that day for the show, so I can recommend the Bunse March Brown Dun with confidence—the trout loved it. These mayflies hatch from morning to midday in early season, disappear in midseason, and then return in fall. The body color of the dun varies between the two species and the location; colors can range from slate to olive to peach to yellow. You can collect samples and match them or use the ochre color Richard prefers. Fly size, presentation, and outline are so far ahead of color in importance that I seldom fret over the latter. There are western march browns, and there are eastern march browns. The easterns are a different genus than the westerns and are similar in color, but slightly larger.

BUNSE MARCH BROWN DUN

HOOK: Short-shank, dry-fly, sizes 18 to 16
(with the foam extension, these hooks will make a fly comparable in size to a conventional one of size 16 or 14; the hook shown is a Mustad 94838).
THREAD: Yellow 6/0 or 8/0.
BODY: Ethafoam sheeting colored with an ocher (dark yellow) marking pen.
TAIL: Two mink-tail, nutria, or beaver guard hairs.
WING: Dark coastal deer hair (brown preferred).

1. Color a piece of ethafoam sheeting. Cut out a blunt-ended, diamond-shaped section from the sheeting about 1 1/4" long by 7/16" wide (slightly over three full hook lengths long by slightly over one hook length wide). Color the edges of the sheeting if you like.

2. Mount a beading needle in your vise as shown. Start the thread lightly near the center of the needle. Using a light turn, tie in the tip of the diamond-shape foam section as shown. The foam should be tied on the far side of the needle. Use light thread tension throughout the needle tying—it will help you remove the foam later.

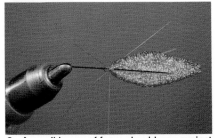

3. A small hump of foam should now project behind the thread. Hold one tail hair above and another below this hump, take a light turn of thread around both hairs. Tighten the turn of thread until the tails spread. Leave the butts of the tails long and untrimmed.

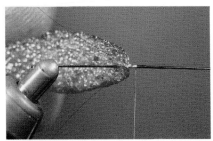

4. Bend back the foam and advance the thread in two or three turns over the needle and tail butts.

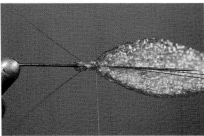

5. Bend the foam forward again and take two turns of thread around it. The turns should be tight enough to form a round foam segment.

6. Continue forming segments, each slightly larger than the last, until there are four (the hump behind the tails counts as a segment). Half hitch the thread, trim it, and slide the body off the needle.

7. Remove the needle from your vise. Mount a hook in your vise, and then start the thread halfway up the shank; comb, stack (stacking is usually optional with coastal deer for all but the smaller hook sizes) and tie in a bunch of coastal deer hair for a wing (the wing should be one-and-a-half times as long as the hook's shank). Trim the wing's butts at an angle and bind them with thread.

8. Remove the hook from your vise. Push the point of the hook through the foam body, where the butts of the tails project, and out around the bottom of the fourth segment (by "bottom" I mean the side that should end up beneath the fly, seam on top). Slide the foam body up the bend to the end of the shank. Return the hook to your vise. Work the thread back to the foam body and take two thread turns around the end of the last segment, where the half hitch holds the body together.

9. Draw the front of the foam down out of the way as you advance the thread to the hook's eye. Catch the tails' butts with the thread; trim the butts near the eye. With your thumbnail, crease the hair wing upright; then pull it back and add a few tight thread turns against its front.

10. With your right hand (right-handers), pull the front of the foam forward and up; then support the foam, forward and up around the sides of the shank, with your left hand; take up the bobbin with your right and secure the tip of the foam at the eye with tight thread turns. Stretch the end of the foam and trim it closely.

11. Spiral the thread back between the wing and the hook's eye and take one full turn of thread. Then spiral the thread *beneath* the wing to the rear of the wing. Take two thread turns here, spiral the thread under the thorax to the front of the wing, take a full turn over the previous full turn, and then work the thread back to the eye.

12. Snip a tiny slit on each side of the foam at the wing's base—but watch that you don't cut the thread.

Thread Wrapping Thorax

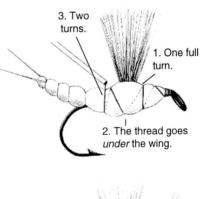

3. Two turns.

1. One full turn.

2. The thread goes *under* the wing.

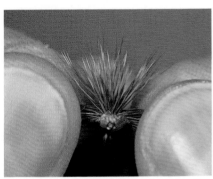

13. Pull the wing down into the side slits, forming a fan wing. Create a thread head, add a whip finish, and trim the thread.

14. Touch up the foam with your marking pen if needed. Add a drop of thinned Flexament (three parts thinner to one part Flexament) to the body just behind the wing; add another at the base of the tails (the rear tip of the body). Add head cement to the thread head. (I usually brush the whole foam body sparingly with the thinned Flexament and, rather than adding head cement, dab some on the thread head).

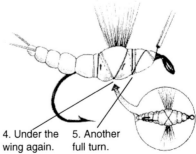

4. Under the wing again.

5. Another full turn.

III

CADDISFLY IMITATIONS

Introduction To Caddisflies

In contrast to the mayfly's life cycle of three stages, the caddisfly has four: the bottom-dwelling larval stage; the surface-seeking pupal stage; the newly hatched, winged adult; and the ovipositing (egg-laying) adult. It is the last two of these stages—the new adult and the ovipositing adult—that most interest the dry-fly fisher and the dry-fly tier.

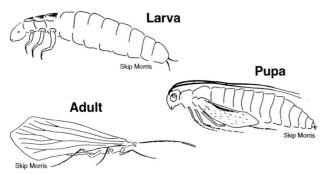

Sometimes caddisflies hit the surface, pop from their shucks, and take wing almost as a single motion; trout figure this out and slash quickly at the new adults the moment they appear. Other caddisflies hatch sedately, and trout take them calmly and rhythmically. The egg-laying female caddisflies usually slap to the surface, dance and dart as they drop their eggs, and then spring again to flight. Trout have little time to respond, so they watch for such flies and take them fiercely.

Like mayflies, caddisflies live in water ranging from silent ponds to the swift runs of mountain streams. Also like mayflies, caddisflies vary dramatically in size and color from species to species.

The adult caddisfly at rest folds its four wings back with the top edges together and the lower edges down along the sides of the body—"tentlike" is the term often used to describe a resting caddis's wings. Long, substantial antennas are another caddis characteristic.

The caddisfly imitations tied in this section serve to suggest all the caddis's varied top-water forms and actions—the Elk Hair Caddis will bounce atop a lively current and skate about at the angler's direction; the Skaddis rests with a silhouette to match the quiet caddisflies around it; and other imitations will do yet other things.

TYING DIFFICULTY
1 is easy; 5 is difficult

Skaddis	2
Elk Hair Caddis	3
Henryville Special	4
CDC Caddis Emerger	4
Goddard Caddis	5

The Skaddis

A true fishing fly—that is, a fly that most fly fishers will tie and fish rather than merely discuss and read about and nothing more—must have the following qualities: It must require, at most, a modest amount of time for the average tier to create, it must be constructed of materials relatively easy to obtain, it must be durable, and it must catch fish at least as well as any other fly of its type. This is my pragmatic and experience-won definition of a true fishing fly, and the Skaddis, in both its light and dark versions, fits it.

The wings of most adult-caddis imitations are tied in near the hook's eye, but I found that this can cause the wing to flare and lose its definition; the short yarn wing of the Skaddis hasn't the length to spread out, so it stays neatly bunched in the shape and position of a real caddis's wings. True, this short yarn wing starts further down the body than

do a real caddis's wings, but that makes no difference because the first bit of a real caddis's wings are tapered fine and are insignificant from the trout's perspective. Beyond this, there is nothing unique about my caddis, but this simple, durable yarn wing that stays neatly in the appropriate shape is enough.

As I'm sure you've guessed by now, the colors and hook size of this fly can be varied to imitate a variety of caddis species. Most of the time, however, I simply stick with the light and dark versions. The Skaddis suggests a resting adult caddis fly and should be fished dead drift with, if appropriate, the slightest occasional twitches. If the current is heavy, if the natural caddis flies are skittering vigorously about the surface, or both, look to one of the bushy, buoyant caddis imitations; but if you are imitating quiet caddis on light riffles or smooth water, try a Skaddis.

SKADDIS LIGHT

HOOK: Standard dry fly, sizes 22 to 8 (the hook shown is a Dai-Riki 305).
THREAD: Tan 8/0 or 6/0.
ABDOMEN: Tan poly dubbing.
WING: Tan poly yarn.
HACKLE: Ginger.
THORAX: Tan poly dubbing.

SKADDIS DARK

HOOK: Standard dry fly, sizes 22 to 8.
THREAD: Brown 8/0 or 6/0.
ABDOMEN: Brown poly dubbing.
WING: Brown poly yarn.
HACKLE: Brown.
THORAX: Brown poly dubbing.

1. Dub a substantial abdomen from the bend up two-thirds of the shank, and then use the pinch to tie in a length of poly yarn ahead of the abdomen as shown. (The thickness of the yarn will depend on the size of the fly; use the photos as a guide.)

2. Snip the butts of the poly yarn at an angle, and then bind them with thread. Tie in a single hackle, trim its stem, and bind the trimmed end with thread.

3. Dub a full thorax, and then palmer the hackle up it in three to five turns. Tie off the hackle and complete the head as usual.

4. Draw the yarn tight and with one quick snip, trim it to wing length. Trim the hackle fibers flat underneath or to a shallow "V." Complete the Skaddis Light by cementing its thread head.

The Elk Hair Caddis

This is Al Troth's ingenious caddis pattern. Al figured out an easy way to wrap a hackle from front to back and reinforce it at the same time. What I like most about the hackle style of the Elk Hair Caddis is that its hackle fibers sweep back and that the shorter fibers are to the rear; all this adds up to a caddis imitation that can really be twitched and skated.

Practically every fly shop now carries the Elk Hair Caddis in an assortment of sizes, and color variations are common. The most popular alternate colors for the Elk Hair Caddis seem to be olive, tan, and black.

Securing the hackle's tip with the gold wire is a problem for some tiers. I prefer to hold the hackle pliers up and back with one hand as I wrap the wire one-half turn with the other; I then release the pliers with the same hand that is holding them as I hold the wire's half turn firmly with the other hand. Another approach is simply to let the pliers hang on the far side of the hook as you handle the wire with both hands. Use whichever method you prefer. The other problem area seems to be the securing of the wing, which is closely related to the forming of the wing-butt head. Be certain that you hold the wing firmly in place as you secure it with plenty of tight thread turns; this and plenty of head cement should keep its position fast. A foundation of tight thread turns can also help to insure a secure wing. The butts of the hair can be trimmed before the wing is tied in (my preference) or after; here again, the choice is yours.

ELK HAIR CADDIS

HOOK: Standard dry fly, sizes 18 to 8 (the hook shown is a Tiemco 900 BL).
THREAD: Tan 3/0 (some tiers prefer standard trout threads, especially for the smaller sizes, but 3/0 allows tight turns that really secure the wing).
RIB: Fine gold wire.
BODY: Hare's mask fur.
HACKLE: One, brown.
WING: Bleached elk hair.

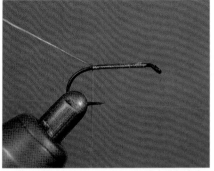

1. Start the thread about 1/16" behind the eye, and then tie in some gold wire. Wrap the thread tightly down the wire to the bend.

2. Dub a full body to about 1/8" short of the eye. Tie in the hackle.

3. Palmer the hackle down the body to the bend in six to ten turns, and then secure the hackle's tip with two or three turns of gold wire.

4. Wrap the wire up through the hackle to the front of the body in roughly the same number of turns as the number of hackle turns. Secure the wire with tight thread turns and trim its end.

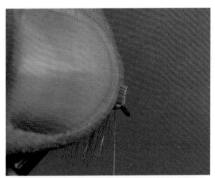

5. Comb and stack a bunch of elk. Tie in the elk using the pinch and add plenty of tight thread turns. I like to hold the stacked hair over the hook with the hair about 1/16" (just slightly) forward of its final position; then I snip the butts straight across at the front tip of the eye, move the trimmed edge to the rear of the eye, and bind the wing. I like the wing to extend *slightly* past the far edge of the bend as shown.

6. Add the whip finish around the *thread collar* (no thread head this time). Trim off the hackle's tip. Add head cement to the collar only.

The Henryville Special

Here is an adult-caddis imitation that has remained popular and productive for many years. And why shouldn't it? It has a clean wing outline, plenty of buoyancy, and enough hackle to allow you to make it skate and skitter.

A traditional tying approach is covered first, but following that is my own approach which requires single-strand floss and a floss bobbin.

The original pattern called for a red floss body, but olive eventually took red's place. Now it is sometimes tied with a dubbed body, and colors other than olive are sometimes substituted: tans, browns, yellows, whatever.

The Henryville Special was created by Hiram Brobst and was christened on the Henryville section of Pennsylvania's Broadhead Creek.

HENRYVILLE SPECIAL

HOOK: Standard dry fly, sizes 20 to 12 (the hook shown is an Eagle Claw D59F).
THREAD: Brown 8/0 or 6/0.
PALMERED RIB: Grizzly hackle (one size smaller than usual).
BODY: Olive floss or dubbing.
UNDER WING: Wood duck or mallard dyed wood-duck color.
WINGS: Natural gray mallard quill.
HACKLE: Brown.

1. Start the thread, tie in a grizzly hackle (one size smaller than usual) at the bend, add dubbing or tie in floss, and wrap a body up two-thirds of the shank. (If you used floss, bind its end and trim it.)

2. Palmer the hackle up the body in about six turns, secure the hackle's tip with thread turns, and trim the tip. Trim the hackle fibers from the top half of the body.

3. Using the pinch, tie in a bunch of fibers from a wood-duck or mallard-dyed-to-wood-duck-color feather atop the body. Trim the butts of the fibers and bind them with thread.

4. Tie in a matched set of quill wings, long edges down, cupped around the wood duck. You can tie both quill sections in at the same time using the wing pinch, but I prefer to tie the quills in down the sides of the body a bit, one at a time.

5. Snip the butts of the quills and bind them with thread. (Note the length of the wings; they can be slightly longer or shorter, but what you see is about right.) Tie in two brown hackles (or only one if you prefer).

6. Wind the first hackle, secure its tip under thread turns, and then wind the second hackle through the first (unless, of course, you are using only one hackle). Secure the second hackle's tip with thread, and then trim both tips. Create a thread head and complete the fly as usual.

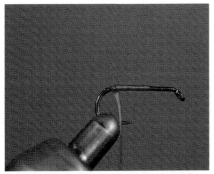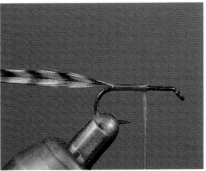

7. My method. Start with single-strand floss in a floss bobbin (here I chose the option of yellow floss). Start the floss two-thirds up the shank as you would thread, and then wrap it back to the bend.

8. Tie in the hackle at the bend with turns of floss. Wrap the floss back to its starting point. Trim the hackle's stem.

9. Wrap the floss forward beyond the body a bit, and then start the tying thread over the end of the floss; wrap the thread back to the floss body in a few tight turns. Trim the ends of both the floss and thread, palmer the hackle forward, and continue tying with the thread as usual.

The CDC Caddis Emerger

Although cul de canard feathers have been used for years by European tiers, "CDC," the common name for these feathers, has only recently been discovered by American tiers. CDC is buoyant and glistens quietly; these are its properties that fly tiers find most significant. A word of advice: do not use floatant on CDC.

Rene' Harrop deserves much of the credit for the rapid evolution of American CDC fly patterns; the Olive CDC Caddis Emerger is one of many Harrop CDC innovations.

There is a growing list of barely dry flies—that is, flies that are meant to be fished partly sunk—and the Olive CDC Caddis Emerger is on that list. This fly is normally fished dead drift, but Rene' tells me that by casting gently and as little as possible, the CDC wing will pick up enough water to allow the fly to sink; then the Olive CDC Caddis

Emerger can be coaxed across the current ever so quietly, in the same manner as a Soft Hackle is fished, to deadly effect—versatile fly. Olive is, of course, only one of many color schemes that can be used with the CDC Caddis Emerger.

OLIVE CDC CADDIS EMERGER

HOOK: Standard dry fly, sizes 20 to 14 (the hook shown is a Daiichi 1170).
THREAD: Olive 8/0 or 6/0.
RIB: Medium gold wire.
ABDOMEN: Dubbing blend of chopped olive angora goat and olive rabbit or mohair.
COLLAR: Partridge or speckled hen fibers, sparse.
WINGS: Two olive CDC tips.
ANTENNAE: Two wood-duck fibers (or mallard dyed wood-duck color).
THORAX: Same dubbing as body but of charcoal-gray color.

1. Start the thread at midshank. Tie in the gold wire and wrap the thread down it to the bend. In your palm, slide a finger across a line of dubbing until you have a dubbing rope.

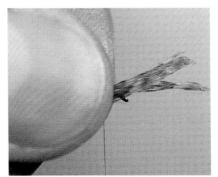

2. Tie in the dubbing rope (but tie in the dubbing a bit up from its tip so that some of it trails off the bend to represent part of a caddisfly's shuck).

3. Spin the rope tightly around the thread, and then wrap this rope-thread up two-thirds of the shank. (The tightly wound dubbing should create a segmented effect.)

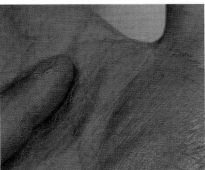

4. Wrap the wire as a rib up the segmented abdomen; the wire should drop into the depressions. Secure the wire and trim its end. Add partridge-feather fibers as a sparse collar; the fibers should reach to the rear end of the abdomen. Rene' spins on the fibers as deer hair is spun, but I've had my best luck by holding a section of fibers flat over the abdomen, bringing the thumb and finger of my other hand down to slide the fibers down around the sides of the abdomen, and then taking a few turns of thread to tie in the fibers' butts.

5. The thumb and finger lowered, bringing the fibers down around the abdomen.

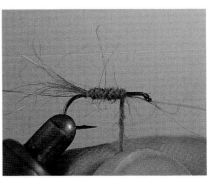

6. Tie in two CDC feather tips curving away from one another; the tips should reach to the rear edge of the abdomen. You can hold the feathers over the abdomen with one hand, as shown, and then use the other hand to lower the feathers to the hook and perform the pinch. Trim the feathers' and partridge fibers' butts and bind them with thread.

7. Tie in two wood-duck fibers atop the hook as antennae; these should extend to about the rear edge of the *hook*. Dub the thorax. Create the usual thread head.

The Goddard Caddis

A bit further on in this book you will find a section titled "Rough Water Flies"; the Goddard Caddis floats so well that it could just as easily be there as here. American Andre Puyans, Englishman John Goddard, and a fishing companion of Goddard's, Cliff Henry, discovered an excuse to form a huge, buoyant deer-hair body on a caddisfly imitation. The excuse—a fine one—is that this great bulge of deer hair, when properly shaped, forms a precise caddis outline, wings and all. So the Goddard Caddis floats high and long and offers a convincing appearance. Clever.

The original Goddard Caddis has antennas, but I consider them optional and I don't bother with them unless I am tying a Goddard Caddis for display.

GODDARD CADDIS

HOOK: Standard dry fly, sizes 16 to 8 (the hook shown is a Partridge L3A).
THREAD: Brown 8/0 or 6/0; for the deer, I like to use gray size-A rod-winding thread.
WING AND BODY: Natural gray deer hair (or caribou) spun, packed, and trimmed to shape.
HACKLE: Brown.
ANTENNAS: (Optional) brown hackle stems stripped of fibers.

1. Start the size-A thread at the bend and use just enough tight turns to get the thread securely fastened. Comb a bunch of deer hair, snip off its tips, and hold the bunch atop the hook's bend. Take two loose turns of thread around the bunch; then work the bunch down around the shank. Hold the hair bunch firmly in place as you pull the thread tight.

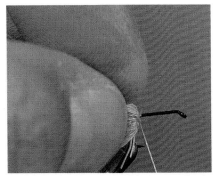

2. Maintain thread tension as you firmly draw back the hair and add four tight thread turns at the hair's base.

3. Spin on a smaller bunch of deer; compress both hair bunches together. Continue spinning on and compressing smaller and smaller bunches (a total of as few as two for small hooks and up to four on large hooks) until slightly over half the shank is covered. (See "Spinning Deer Hair" in section X, "Basic Techniques".)

4. Whip finish the thread. Remove the hook from your vise and sight down the front of the hook as you make your first cut along the underside of the spun hair. Cut close, but not too close! (In the photograph, I'm holding the hook in an old set of fly-vise jaws—my favorite method.) (See "Shaping Spun Hair" in section X, "Basic Techniques.")

5. With scissors, a razor blade, or both, trim the body-wing to a wedge shape. The large end of the wedge should slant as shown.

6. Top view of the body-wing.

7. Replace the hook in your vise, and then start some 8/0 or 6/0 thread over the end of the size-A thread. Tie in two hackles, and then wrap one and secure its tip with tight thread turns. Wind the second hackle through the first and secure its tip. Trim both tips. Add stripped-hackle-stem antennas if you like. Finish with a thread head and the usual steps.

IV

STONEFLY IMITATIONS

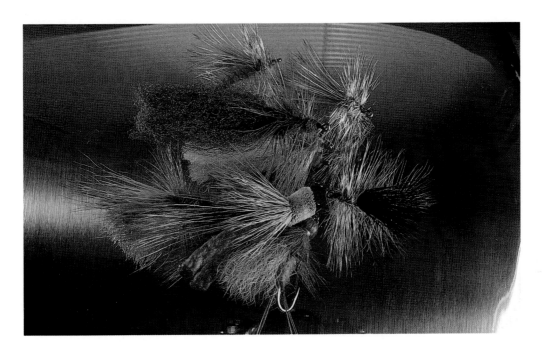

Introduction To Stoneflies

In the West, the very mention of the word "stone-flies" fills anglers' minds with images of huge, clumsy, corpulent insects bobbing among the slashings of great trout. It *can* actually happen that way...almost. But even when the action is only modest and steady, the chance at a big trout on a dry fly is very real when golden stoneflies and salmon flies are hatching. The salmon-fly hatch is legendary; but the golden stones are only a shade smaller, hatch in about the same numbers as the salmons, create just as much excitement with the trout, and are, between the two, by far the more common. Other stones can be important in the West—the little yellow stone, little green stone, and the winter stone to name a few.

Stoneflies are sometimes important in the East; in fact, many stonefly species are found across the United States.

Smaller stoneflies are often imitated with caddisfly patterns. The Elk Hair Caddis, Delta Wing Caddis, and others are all good choices for small-stone hatches—but remember, stoneflies tend to run large, so even a fly small by stonefly standards may be a trout's mouthful.

Characteristically, stoneflies live in moving water, swift usually. They hatch by creeping to the edges of a stream and then crawling out onto rocks or wood to shed their shucks. It is the female adult's clumsy and dangerous ovipositing flight that interests the dry-fly fisher.

Stoneflies hold their wings flat over their bodies. Stoneflies also have prominent tails and antennas in contrast to mayflies, which have prominent tails but almost nonexistent antennas, and caddisflies, which have prominent antennas but lack tails altogether.

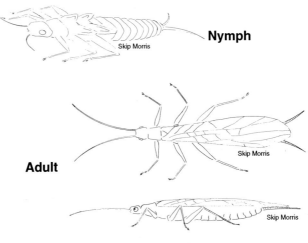

Nymph

Adult

TYING DIFFICULTY
1 is easy; 5 is difficult

Clark's Stonefly	3
Skipping Stone	3
Stimulator	4
Matt's Adult Stone	4
Golden Rod	4

The Clark's Stonefly

I had heard about this fly and had paid it little attention, but when a shadow-box maker asked me to tie him an Oregon fly series and insisted on including the Clark's Stonefly, I began to take notice. Shortly after, I ran into a young man on a tiny creek and was pleasantly surprised to see that he was a fly fisher. I was even more surprised when he mentioned that he was "doing well on a Clark's Stonefly." Stoneflies were coming off the creek, so a stonefly imitation made sense, but there was that Clark's Stonefly again—I suddenly felt I'd been missing something. I'd met Lee Clark once when we were both working a fly-tying exposition, so I gave him a call and found out more about his fly. Since then I've been hearing more and more about the Clark's Stonefly; so even though it is a regional fly pattern, I have included it in this broad-interest book because it is really catching on, it is popping up in fishing magazines, and it works.

Here is a switch from the usual approach to stonefly imitation; its tinsel-and-trailing-yarn body makes the Clark Stonefly unique. Lee uses and sells the macrame yarn called for, but poly yarn substitutes well.

CLARK'S STONEFLY

HOOK: Long shank, dry fly (Lee prefers the Eagle Claw Lazer Sharp L58 size 10 shown, even though it is actually a sunk-fly hook).
THREAD: Yellow or orange 3/0.
BODY: Flat gold mylar tinsel.
UNDERWING (overbody): Lee's Tying Yarn (macrame yarn) or substitute poly yarn. Orange, rust, or both mixed for the salmon fly; orange, gold, or gold and rust mixed for the golden stone.
WING: Natural gray-brown deer or elk hair.
HACKLE: Brown (Lee prefers a single saddle hackle).

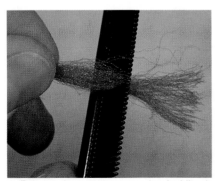

1. Prepare the macrame yarn by doubling it and then combing it out in about five strokes.

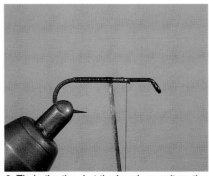

2. Tie in the tinsel at the bend, wrap it up the shank, secure its end with thread turns, and trim the end of the tinsel (or tie in the tinsel up the shank; then wrap it to the bend and back).

3. Using the pinch, tie in the yarn over the tinsel body as you would tie in a wing. Trim the butts of the yarn at an angle and bind them with thread. Trim the yarn to about 1/4" beyond the far edge of the hook's bend.

4. Using the pinch, tie in the deer or elk wing over the yarn (Lee doesn't stack the hair) with tight thread turns. The tips of the wing should extend past the trimmed end of the yarn. Gather the wing with moderate-tension thread turns at the front of the body. Trim the wing's butts at an angle and bind them with thread.

5. Tie in and then wrap a hackle (if you don't have a saddle hackle, a good neck hackle should do). Build a long, thick thread head (Lee's preference); whip finish and trim the thread; add head cement.

6. Trimming the hackle's underside to a "V" is optional.

The Skipping Stone

After discovering the twisted-yarn extended body and the toughness and buoyancy of poly yarn, it wasn't long before the first Skipping Stone was locked in my vise. The trick with adult-stonefly imitations is getting the fly's body down onto the water while keeping the fly afloat in tumbling stonefly currents. A short hook and a buoyant extended body seemed just the combination; it was. Besides, I believe that soft materials enhance a fly's ability to hook fish, so you will see this philosophy followed in my flies whenever possible, the Skipping Stone included.

The twisted-yarn body is quite simple to create—just twist the yarn in two different directions until it doubles. If you use the hook in your vise to tug at the twisted yarn, the spot where the hook tugs will be the spot where the yarn doubles; this gives you control. If, however, the yarn has a kink where it was folded around the card it came on, that is where it will want to fold. You have the option of using a hook with a longer shank than the one on the Daiichi hook shown. A longer shank will stretch out the thorax which will add more orange to the Skipping Stone Salmon Fly, and a longer shank can be helpful if trout are nipping at the fly or seizing only part of it—the more hook, the more likely a nip will find it. On the other hand, a short shank minimizes hook and maximizes buoyancy. It's all trade-offs really; let experience and common sense prevail. A conversation with John Hazel, who guides and teaches fly fishing on the Deschutes River, convinced me to experiment with subtle colors in the abdomen of my Skipping Stone Salmon Fly. He says that by the time the adult stones are dancing on the river, they are much more somber than at first emergence.

There are two versions of the Skipping Stone: Salmon Fly and Golden. Fish both dead drift or with twitches during the spring-summer salmon-fly and golden-stone hatches in the West.

SKIPPING STONE GOLDEN

HOOK: Short shank, dry fly; because of the extended body,
size depends partly on hook design and personal
choice; usually I end up with about a size 10 or 8.
The bodies of most adult golden stones are 1 to 1
1/2 inches. (The hook shown is a Daiichi 1640).
THREAD: Tan 3/0.
ABDOMEN: Gold poly yarn.
WING: Tan poly yarn (brown is better when imitating some
golden stones).
HACKLE: One, ginger.
THORAX: Gold poly dubbing.
HEAD: Ball of gold poly dubbing.

SKIPPING STONE SALMON FLY

HOOK: Short shank, dry fly; because of the extended
body, size depends on hook design and personal
choice; usually, I end up with about a size 8 or 6.
The bodies of adult salmon flies are about 1 1/2 to 2
inches.
THREAD: Orange 3/0.
ABDOMEN: Brown poly yarn, twisted.
WING: Brown poly yarn.
HACKLE: One, dark brown.
THORAX: Orange poly dubbing.
HEAD: Brown poly dubbing.

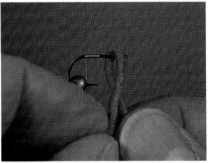

1. Start the thread at midshank and spiral it tightly to the bend. Twist the ends of a section of poly yarn in opposite directions; then tug the yarn against the hook to make the yarn double on itself. Stroke the twisted yarn if necessary to straighten it.

2. Secure the twisted yarn at the bend with tight thread turns—be certain you don't lose the twist in the yarn. The best way I have found to secure the twisted yarn is to use a "reverse pinch," with the hands switched as shown. Trim the yarn's butts at an angle and bind the butts with tight thread turns.

3. Use the pinch to secure a section of poly yarn at the bend; trim its butt at an angle and bind it with thread turns. Secure a single hackle at the bend.

4. Dub a full thorax, but leave enough space for a dubbing head, and then palmer the hackle up the thorax in five to eight turns.

5. Create a dubbed head; then create a thread head and complete it as usual.

6. Snip the wing fibers to length—just past the end of the body like the wings of a real stonefly. Snip a shallow "V" in the hackle's underside.

7. A Skipping Stone Golden tied on a hook with a standard-length shank.

The Stimulator

Randall Kaufmann has developed a number of effective western fly patterns, and of those, the Stimulator is probably the most-tied and most-fished. Here is a straightforward adult-stonefly imitation that sees a lot of duty on western streams. The Green Stimulator tied here imitates not only various greenish stoneflies, but greenish caddisflies as well; the Yellow Stimulator imitates yellow stoneflies such as *Isoperla,* and the Black Stimulator is strictly an imitation of the huge stonefly commonly referred to as the salmon fly. Stimulators can also be used as "attractor" flies, flies that draw strikes not by imitation, but by simply suggesting something alive, plump, and edible.

If the elk-hair wing is too thick, you will have trouble handling the thorax. The wing in the photos is the *thickest* I would advise, but you can make a wing considerably thinner and still have a good fly. Goat is coarse dubbing; chopping it up with your scissors helps make it easy to handle, as does a liberal application of wax to the thread.

GREEN STIMULATOR

HOOK: Long shank, dry fly, sizes 18 to 10 (Randall prefers the Tiemco 200 shown in the photographs).
THREAD: Orange or fluorescent orange 8/0, 6/0 or 3/0 (I suggest 3/0 for all but the smallest sizes).
TAIL: Gray elk hair.
RIB: One brown hackle palmered down the abdomen and counter ribbed with fine gold wire.
ABDOMEN: Bright-green or olive Haretron.
WING: Gray elk hair.
THORAX: Amber goat.
HACKLE: One grizzly palmered up the thorax.

YELLOW STIMULATOR

HOOK: Long shank, dry fly, sizes 18 to 6 (Randall prefers
the Tiemco 200 shown in the photographs).
THREAD: Red or fluorescent orange 8/0, 6/0, or 3/0
(I suggest 3/0 for all but the smallest sizes).
TAIL: Light natural elk.
RIB: One furnace or brown hackle counter ribbed with fine
gold wire.
ABDOMEN: Bright-yellow Haretron or Antron dubbing.
WING: Light natural elk.
THORAX: Amber goat.
HACKLE: One grizzly hackle palmered up the thorax.

BLACK STIMULATOR

HOOK: Long shank, dry fly, sizes 8 and 6 (Randall prefers
the Tiemco 200 shown in the photographs).
THREAD: Orange or fluorescent orange 3/0.
TAIL: Black elk hair.
RIB: One dark blue-dun hackle counter-ribbed with fine
gold wire.
ABDOMEN: Blackish blend of angora goat—black, purple,
claret, rust, orange, (I sometimes substitute black
only) and black Haretron.
WING: Black elk hair.
THORAX: Bright- or fluorescent-orange antron.
HACKLE: One grizzly palmered up thorax.

1. Stack and comb a bunch of elk hair; start the thread about two-thirds up the shank. Tie in the elk hair, spiral the thread down the hair and shank to the bend, tie in some gold wire, trim the hair's butts. The elk tail should be short, a gape's length.

2. Dub a body up about two-thirds of the shank. Tie in the brown hackle.

3. Palmer the hackle to the bend, secure its tip with two or three turns of wire, and then spiral the wire forward through the hackle (see "The Elk Hair Caddis," same approach to hackling). Trim the hackle's tip.

4. Comb and stack another bunch of elk and, using the pinch, tie it in as a wing; this wing should extend to the far edge of the hook's bend. Trim the wing's butts at an angle and bind them with thread.

5. Tie in the grizzly hackle, and then dub the thorax.

6 Palmer the hackle up the thorax in about four turns. Finish the fly with a thread head and the usual steps.

The Matt's Adult Stone

Fly tiers have discovered woven polypropylene macrame chord during the last few years, and the Matt's Adult Stonefly makes wise use of this promising new material. I found the Matt's Adult Stone in *Fly Patterns of Yellowstone* by Craig Mathews and John Juracek. Shortly after that I discovered a very similar pattern by Al Troth called the MacSalmon (listed in section XVII, "Additional Dry Flies"). Use whichever you like; both are tied in similar fashion.

Elk mane is excellent for the wing because it has length, density, and flexibility. If you can't get elk mane, Craig says that deer mane is a good substitute; if both of these were unavailable, I would probably choose red-fox squirrel tail.

Fish the Matt's Adult Stone as you would any stonefly imitation—dead drift or with an occasional twitch or skid.

MATT'S ADULT STONE

> *HOOK*: Standard dry fly, sizes 8 to 4 (the hook shown is a Gamakatsu F-11-B).
> *THREAD*: 3/0 to match body color; gray or white size-A rod-winding thread for spinning the deer hair.
> *BODY*: Orange, gold, or yellow woven polypropylene macrame chord.
> *WING*: Elk mane or substitute; wing butts covered with dubbing of the same color as the body.
> *COLLAR*: Deer-hair tips.
> *HEAD*: Deer hair spun and trimmed to shape.

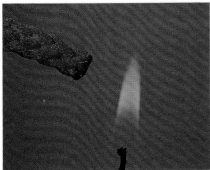

1. Snip a short section of poly chord and touch a flame to its cut end until the fibers melt together into a dark stub; this will keep the cord from unraveling.

2. Start the 3/0 thread and tie in the cord at midshank using the pinch; the cord should project from its tie-in point about one full hook's length or slightly more. Trim the chord's butt at an angle and bind the fibers under tight thread wraps.

3. Comb and stack a bunch of elk-mane hair and, using the pinch, tie it in as a wing ahead of the body's tie-in point. The tips of the elk should extend a bit past the end of the body. Trim the hair's butts at an angle and bind them with thread. Using fur or poly dubbing of the body's color, dub over the thread-bound hair butts.

4. Whip finish the 3/0 thread and start the size-A. Comb and stack a bunch of deer hair and tie it in as a collar; the hair's tips should reach about halfway down the body. (See "Spinning Deer Hair" in section X, "Basic Techniques.")

5. Comb, spin on, and compress more deer hair (one or two bunches should do) until the hair reaches the eye. Whip finish and trim the thread.

6. Shape the deer-hair head with scissors or a razor blade (see "Shaping Spun Hair" in section X, "Basic Techniques"). The head, as shown, should have a blunt, tapered shape; the underside of the head should be trimmed close to the shank and the underside of the collar should be trimmed away. Add head cement to the *thread* head.

The Goldenrod

My friend Rod Robbinson developed this imitation of the golden stonefly after years of playing with variations. The testing ground was Oregon's Metolius River, a swift spring creek with a golden-stone hatch stretching from May well into September. Odd for a hatch that only lasts two or three weeks on the nearby Deschutes River, but for developing a golden-stone imitation the Metolius's long hatch offered a fine opportunity. The name "Goldenrod" is my own. "It has to have a name if I'm going to write about it," I told Rod, and since he had none, he allowed mine to stand.

What makes the Goldenrod unique is its foam core, made from a piece of a foam cup, which provides a lot of buoyancy. Rod likes to poke Goldenrods well back under cut banks and overhanging brush and branches.

GOLDENROD

HOOK: Long shank, dry fly, size 8 (the hook shown is a Daiichi 1270).
THREAD: Tan or gold 8/0, 6/0, or 3/0 (I prefer the 3/0).
TAILS: Pheasant-tail fibers split around a ball of dubbing.
CORE: Section of foam cup.
ABDOMEN AND THORAX: Gold poly dubbing.
HACKLE: One brown.
WING: Calf tail dyed tan.
HEAD AND COLLAR: Gold-dyed elk hair (if you can't find gold, substitute natural tan; deer hair is fragile, so it is your last choice).

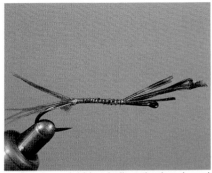

1. Create a dubbing ball at the bend, and then tie in one group of three or four pheasant-tail fibers on either side as tails. Spiral the thread tightly up three-quarters of the shank and trim the tails' butts.

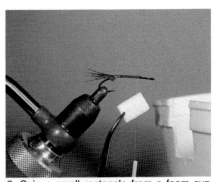

2. Snip a small rectangle from a foam cup and wrap it around the shank just ahead of the tails; the rectangle should wrap once around the shank and should reach from just ahead of the tails to three-quarters up the shank. If the foam rectangle breaks as you wrap it, no problem.

3. Bind the foam to the shank with thread turns. Control the abdomen's diameter by the tightness of the thread wraps, but remember—compression squeezes out the foam's air and with it, buoyancy.

4. Dub to midshank, tie in a hackle, and dub to the front of the foam. Palmer the hackle up the dubbed foam in three to five turns; secure the hackle's tip with thread turns and trim the tip.

5. Trim a "V" in the top of the hackle. Comb and stack a bunch of calf-tail hair and tie it in as a wing so that it lays in the hackle's "V." Trim the butts of the calf at an angle and bind them with thread turns.

6. Wrap the thread to just behind the eye. Comb and stack a bunch of elk, slip its butts over the eye, secure it with tight thread turns right behind the eye, and bind its butts with thread. The thread should hang slightly ahead of the front of the body. (See "Bullet Head" in section X, "Basic Techniques.")

7. Draw the hair back as a bullet head and bind it with a thread collar. Whip finish the collar and trim the thread. Turn the fly upside down and trim the hair tips and hackle from the fly's underside. Add head cement to the thread collar only.

V

TERRESTRIAL IMITATIONS

Introduction To Terrestrials

The term "terrestrials," when used by fly fishers, refers to insects that live on land—no part of their life cycles includes living in water. Because terrestrials often end up awash and available to trout, they are important to the fly fisher. The grasshopper is big and apparent, and it is the terrestrial most anglers think of first. Add to the grasshopper the ant and beetle and you have what must surely be the day in-day out top-three terrestrials.

In certain places at certain times other terrestrial insects may have the full and singular attention of the trout—I have seen trout slash eagerly at spiders that skimmed across a western lake on silver strands of web, and Roderick Haig-Brown wrote about "a Canadian day" of storm and lightning during which he suddenly hooked seven trout in quick succession and upon opening some up found them "full of bees, beautiful brown honey bees" that he "supposed the storm had beaten to the water."

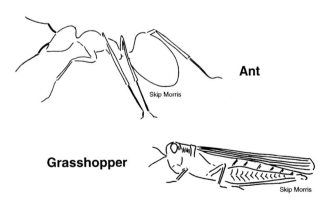

Ant

Skip Morris

Grasshopper

Skip Morris

My own first experience with trout and terrestrials came the summer of my eighteenth birthday. As a graduation gift, I requested and was granted a two-week fishing trip to Montana. There was no resistance—in light of my grades, my graduation was viewed as a cause for celebra-

tion, a miracle. This was an excellent time to make requests. I should probably have asked for the whole summer in New Zealand.

My companions and I drove quickly to Montana and began fishing on the first stream whose name we recognized; that stream was the Bitterroot River. I'd read about the Bitterroot, but I had no idea how drastically some rivers are drawn down for irrigation—though its bed was broad and well defined, there lay only a scant flow connecting shallow open pools only a fly rod or two across.

I had noticed a few grasshoppers so I put on a Joe's Hopper—the standard grasshopper imitation of that day. The first pool was shallow and mostly placid. I tossed in the fly and waited; a bulge appeared and my fly was gone. I set the hook in what proved to be a two-pound brown trout. When I later opened it up, it was as full of grasshoppers as Haig-Brown's trout had been full of honey bees.

There I was on my first Montana stream with my first brown trout, the trout so admired for its cunning and caution and reluctance to take an artificial fly—and such a huge trout—and I had chosen just the fly that would catch it (by little more than luck). I was proud indeed, and for the first time I was not only relieved, but actually glad that I had graduated from high school.

TYING DIFFICULTY
1 is easy; 5 is difficult

Foam Beetle	1
Black Ant	2
Letort Hopper	3
Henry's Fork Hopper	5
Jay-Dave's Hopper	5

The Foam Beetle

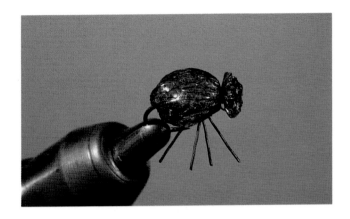

There are a number of foam-beetle variations—once sheets of buoyant, flexible foam became easily available to fly tiers, beetle imitations made from foam were inevitable and seemed to spring from everywhere. There are lots of fly-tying foams on the market, so use whichever you prefer. "Ethafoam" is a foam sheeting that electronics, camera lenses, and such come wrapped in. If you use ethafoam, color it with a waterproof marking pen and then coat the color with highly thinned Dave's Flexament.

(Ethafoam is shown in the tying-sequence photographs.)

The Foam Beetle is durable; the elk-hair legs enhance this durability as they are considerably tougher than deer hair. There is also a new, very fine rubber hackle (rubber legs) that I can't yet seem to obtain in black, but that will probably be available soon; it should make excellent Foam Beetle legs. Other synthetics may also prove good for beetle legs. A similar beetle pattern uses poly yarn for the shell back.

FOAM BEETLE

HOOK: Standard dry fly, sizes 20 to 12 (the hook shown is a Dai-Riki 305).
THREAD: Black 8/0 or 6/0.
LEGS: Dyed-black elk hairs.
SHELL BACK: Black foam strip.

1. Cut a strip of foam about as wide as the hook's shank (this will create a very full shape in the final body, almost round; for a slimmer beetle, cut the strip thinner; experiment). Tie in the foam strip at the bend.

2. At midshank, tie in three to five elk hairs and crisscross the thread at their tie-in point. Make these crisscrossed turns tight enough to flare the hairs apart.

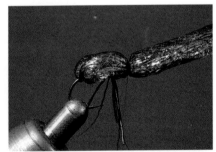

3. Advance the thread three-quarters of the way up the shank. Pull the foam strip up and then down under moderate tension. Secure it with several tight thread turns.

4. To complete the Foam Beetle trim the foam, trim the elk-hair legs, and whip finish and cement the thread collar.

The Black Ant, Cinnamon Ant and Black Flying Ant

From midseason on, there is a good chance that trout in your favorite stream may be hanging close to over-hanging grasses and tree limbs for a chance at a fallen ant. Black ants are the standard, but brown ants, imitated by the Cinnamon Ant, are sometimes predominant.

Flying ants are another matter—they can end up all over a stream or lake. The first time I encountered flying ants was on a lake near my parents' home in western Washington. The lake held both bass and rainbow trout, and whichever fish was most active got my attention. I had noticed flying ants on the wing all that evening and had seen plenty on the water, but the bass fishing around the edges was good, and the trout weren't yet showing.

There was a casual rise about 50 feet out from shore. I ignored it and continued to toss a hair bug around sunken logs until the rise repeated three more times; then I could no longer resist. I added a fine tippet to my leader, put on a regular ant pattern (I had no flying-ant imitations), and dropped it neatly (and luckily) near the rise. The fish took confidently, calmly; the whole process had been pretty and efficient and as I tightened on him I felt like quite a fish-erman. He then made a strong dive but with more strength than speed, and I was surprised because most Pear Lake rainbows jump or run long, swiftly, and shallow when they feel the hook. At the boat my rainbow was a bass. Throughout the evening I took bass after bass as they rose like trout all over the lake.

But flying ants attract trout too. In *The Western Angler*, Roderick Haig-Brown wrote, "Somewhere about the first of June—this year it was on May 19th—there is a hot, bright day, and the flying ants are everywhere....They (the trout) rise well to the hatch, either in the tidal water or up in the pools, but they are particular about artificials, probably because the natural is so abundant." "They" refers specifically to sea-running cutthroat trout. Bass, sea-run cutthroat, and probably most fish that will feed on the surface: when the flying ants are out, you may be surprised at what takes your fly.

Ant and flying-ant imitations are generally fished dead drift. Sometimes the tiniest twitch to suggest the insect's struggling may convince a fish.

BLACK ANT

HOOK: Standard dry fly, sizes, 20 to 14 (the hook shown is
     an Eagle Claw D57).
THREAD: Black 8/0 or 6/0.
ABDOMEN: Black dubbing.
HACKLE: Black.
THORAX: Black dubbing.

CINNAMON ANT

HOOK: Standard dry fly, sizes 16 to 20.
THREAD: Brown 8/0 or 6/0.
ABDOMEN: Brown dubbing.
HACKLE: Brown.
THORAX: Brown dubbing.

BLACK FLYING ANT

HOOK: Standard dry fly, sizes 18 to 10.
THREAD: Black 8/0 or 6/0.
ABDOMEN: Black dubbing.
WINGS: Two black hen-neck hackle points.
HACKLE: Brown or black.
THORAX: Black dubbing.

1. Dub a ball over the rear half of the shank.

2. Tie a hackle in just behind the shank's center and wrap it forward in three or four turns. Secure the hackle's tip with thread turns and trim the tip.

3. Dub a second smaller ball of fur at the front of the shank. Whip finish the thread *behind* the front ball of fur and ahead of the hackle. (You can also wrap the hackle, dub the thorax, and then add a thread head at the eye, but the method I've described really defines and separates the abdomen and thorax.) Add head cement to the whip finish.

4. By adding a hackle-tip wing along each side of the abdomen before tying in the hackle, the Black Ant becomes the Black Flying Ant.

The Letort Hopper and The Letort Cricket

Compared with the other hopper flies explored in this section, this hopper might seem unfinished and primitive; but Ed Shenk, legend of the Pennsylvania limestone streams, knew what he was doing when he created the Letort Hopper. Any trout willing to take a basic simulation of a grasshopper—and Ed, among others, has proved that that includes some extremely cautious trout—will take a Letort Hopper. Though it is a simple fly, consider what it offers: good body and wing outlines, deer-hair tips to suggest forelegs and jumping legs, and a large deer-hair head much like the head of a real hopper. And with all that this pattern offers trout, it offers the tier an easy time at the vise. Ed Shenk concocted the Letort Cricket shortly after the Letort Hopper. Both flies are tied in the same manner, and all that can be said of the Letort Hopper can be said of the Letort Cricket.

There isn't much to say about the tying of these flies, because they are so simple. You can use 3/0 thread or size-A rod-winding thread; I almost always use size-A for flaring hair. You can toughen the wing with Flexament, Tuffilm, or the like which will enhance durability.

LETORT HOPPER

HOOK: Long shank, dry fly, sizes 16 to 10 (the hook shown
　　　is a Partridge L3A).
THREAD: Gray, yellow, or white 3/0 or size-A rod-winding
　　　thread.
BODY: Yellow dubbing.
WING: Mottled turkey quill section.
HEAD AND COLLAR: Natural deer hair.

LETORT CRICKET

HOOK: Long shank, dry fly, sizes 16 to 10.
THREAD: Black 3/0 or size-A rod-winding thread.
BODY: Black dubbing.
WING: Dyed-black goose or turkey-quill section.
HEAD AND COLLAR: Black deer hair.

1. Dub a thick body up two-thirds of the shank. Trim a section of turkey quill to a short point.

2. Tie the turkey section in atop, and rolled around the sides of, the body; the turkey section should extend just past the rear end of the hook. Trim the butts of the section.

3. Over the wing, atop the body, tie in a bunch of stacked deer hair, tips reaching to the tip of the turkey section.

4. Now you have two choices: You can spin and compress another batch of deer hair in front of the butts of the first batch (see "Spinning Deer Hair" in section X, "Basic Techniques"), or you can wind the thread forward through the butts of the first batch which will spread the butts enough for a head. The two-bunch method is slowest, but creates the densest head. Create a thread head and add head cement. Whip finish the thread, trim it, shape the spun-hair head, and add head cement to the whip finish.

The Henry's Fork Hopper

Since its creation, the Henry's Fork Hopper has been on a steady rise of popularity. Tie it, fish it—you'll see why.

The extended body that suggests a real grasshopper's humped rump is difficult to execute for some tiers. The section titled "The Paradrake" offers lots of guidelines for handling extended hair bodies. I use my usual epoxy head cement to treat the wing, but I have to tie in the wing at the point when the epoxy is firmly set but not yet at full hardness, usually between six and fifteen hours. Dave's Flexament and vinyl cement also create a tough wing. I've seen both knotted pheasant-tail fibers and the treated pheasant feathers pictured used to suggest the Henry's Fork Hopper's big jumping legs; use whichever you like. Al Troth's rubber-strand hopper legs described in "Jay-Dave's Hopper" would also be good here.

The Henry's Fork Hopper was created by Mike Lawson.

HENRY'S FORK HOPPER

HOOK: Long shank, dry fly, sizes 12 to 8 (the hook shown is a Tiemco 5212).
THREAD: Yellow 3/0.
BODY: Light-colored or dyed-yellow elk hair.
UNDERWING: Yellow elk.
WING: Pheasant church-window or hen-saddle feather coated with cement.
LEGS: Knotted pheasant-tail fibers.
HEAD AND COLLAR: Natural-gray elk hair

1. Comb (no need to stack) a bunch of elk hair, trim its tips, and tie it in by its cut tips at the bend using the pinch.

2. Wrap down the hair extending off the hook, add three tight thread turns in one place, and then work the thread back to the bend and onto the hook. You can reverse the hook in your vise as shown which can make this step easier; if you do reverse it, return it to its original position when this step is finished.

3. Push your finger straight into the hair to flare it. Divide the hair in half. Pull one half forward on each side, stroke the hairs to even them, and tie down the hairs at the bend. (You can tie in the halves one at a time if you find that easier.)

4. Rib the thread up the hair and then secure the hair about three-quarters up the shank. Trim the hairs butts closely.

5. Comb, stack, and use the pinch to tie in the underwing, which should reach back to about the end of the extended body. Work the thread back one rib turn and gather the wing with a moderate-tension thread turn. Trim closely the underwing's butts.

6. Strip the fuzz from the base of a pheasant church-window or hen-saddle feather and coat it with Dave's Flexament, and then draw the feather between your thumb and finger to create the wing. It is wise to do a number of feathers at once, in advance of tying hoppers.

7. Roll the wing over the top of the body and secure it with two moderate-tension turns one rib back from where the wing will be secured. Secure the wing forward with tight thread wraps; trim the feather's stem if necessary.

8. The Henry's Fork Hopper is often tied without kicker legs, but if you wish them, tie them in now (see "The Jay-Dave's Hopper").

9. Comb, stack, and tie in a bunch of elk hair just behind the eye. Trim closely and thread bind the butts.

0. Draw back the hair and secure it tightly for a bullet head. Trim the kicker legs to length if you chose to add them. Whip finish the thread collar and add head cement to it.

The Jay-Dave's Hopper

It started as the Dave's Hopper, but with Dave Whitlock's permission, Jay Buckner added knotted pheasant-tail legs and thus was born the Jay-Dave's Hopper. Both tiers made significant contributions through this fly: The original Dave's Hopper shifted the thinking towards realism in grasshopper imitation; and Jay Buckner's knotted pheasant-tail legs are so much the standard for grasshopper flies that many fly shops now offer the fibers already knotted. Rubber-strand hopper legs, a new option, are durable and easy to create; an idea from Al Troth.

Knotting pheasant-tail fibers is the step that throws most people. The simplest method I've found employs a knotted loop of leader; illustrations and instructions for this are provided. Tying in the wing securely and well down around the body is another trouble spot; lighter thread turns, back from the tight ones that really hold the wing, will keep the wing down. (If you have trouble working the head and collar into the front quarter of the shank, leave a full third by covering only two-thirds of the shank with the body.) Start the size-A thread in front of the body. As with many other hoppers, this one has a red tail; as I've never seen a live hopper with one, I often omit the tail. The bunch of yellow deer hair under the wing strikes me as optional too.

Fish the Jay-Dave's Hopper as you would any hopper—slap it down, twitch it, throw it low under stream-side grasses—and be prepared for the possibility of a powerful and sudden response.

JAY-DAVE'S HOPPER

HOOK: Long shank, dry fly, sizes 14 to 6 (the hook shown is a Daichii 1270).
THREAD: Yellow 3/0; size-A rod-winding thread for the head and collar.
TAIL: Red deer hair (optional).
BODY: Yellow poly yarn for the body and the loop off the bend.
RIB: Brown hackle, trimmed.
UNDERWING: Yellow deer hair (optional).
WING: Mottled turkey.
LEGS: Knotted pheasant-tail fibers.
HEAD AND COLLAR: Natural-gray deer hair; caribou is good too.

1. Comb, stack, and tie in a deer-hair tail if you like (I don't, but I'll demonstrate in case you do). Tie in the poly yarn three-quarters up the shank, wrap the thread down the yarn and shank to the bend, fold the yarn over into a loop projecting off the bend, secure the yarn (using the pinch) with thread turns.

2. Stroke the fibers out from the sides of a large hackle, and then trim the fibers as shown. Tie in the hackle at the bend. Advance the thread up three-quarters of the shank.

3. Wrap the yarn up three-quarters of the shank, secure its end with thread turns, and trim the yarn. Palmer the hackle up the yarn body. Trim the hackle fibers away on top, at least near the front of the body.

4. Comb, stack, and then tie in a bunch of deer hair over the body; the hairs' tips should reach just past the far end of the yarn loop. (I consider this step optional, but here too, I'll demonstrate.)

5. Trim to round the tip of a turkey-quill section that has been lightly coated with head cement, Dave's Flexament, or sprayed with Tuffilm. Roll the section over the top of the body and secure it with thread turns. Make tight thread turns at the very front of the body to hold the wing secure, and then add a few lighter turns just down the body to bring the wing down into place.

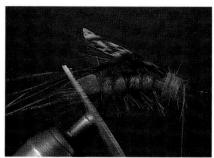

6. Knot two bunches of pheasant-tail fibers as described in the illustration. Tie one bunch on each side of the body as legs. If you like, you can add some yellow dubbing over the thread wraps holding the wing and legs. Trim the tips of the legs to proper length if necessary.

Knotting pheasant-tail Fibers for hopper legs

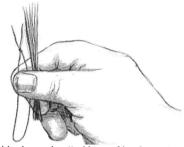

1. Hold a large, knotted loop of leader material and a bunch of pheasant-tail fibers between your thumb and finger as shown.

2. Wrap the fibers once around the base of the loop and then pinch the fibers between your thumb and finger.

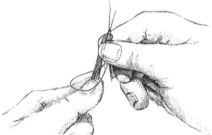

3. Reach through the loop with the thumb and fingers of other hand and grasp the fibers' tips.

4. Grip the leader loops' knot in your teeth and draw the loop up, pulling the fibers' tips up through themselves and creating a knot--keep the knot loose until you've pulled the leader and tips clear throught it; manipulate the knot as needed to accomplish this. Keep a tight grip on the fibers' butts throughout.

5. Pull the loop and fibers from the knot, and then pull the knot tight--legs complete.

7. Switch to the size-A thread. Comb and stack a bunch of deer hair and tie it in as a collar; the hair's tips should reach back about halfway down the body. (See "Spinning Deer Hair" in section X, "Basic Techniques.")

8. Comb, spin on, and compress more deer hair until the hair reaches the eye. Whip finish the thread and trim it. Trim away the collar beneath to expose the body.

9. Trim the hair butts to the shape of a hopper head (see "Shaping Spun Hair" in section X, "Basic Techniques" for instructions on trimming spun hair). Add head cement to the thread head.

10. Rubber-strand legs require three strands still attached to one another. Make a single, tight overhand knot in the strands; then trim away two strands at the knot as shown. Tie in the leg and trim it to length.

VI

TRADITIONAL DRY FLIES

Introduction To Traditional Dry Flies

At one time, the traditional dry fly—bunched tail, two-hackle collar, upright split wings—was the angler's first, second, and third option for rising trout, or trout fishing in general. Prior to that, the wet fly held this spot—but that's another matter. There has been a revolution over the last decade or two—with greater awareness of trout-food insects other than mayflies, which traditional dry flies generally imitate, study and observation have produced patterns that closely mimic insect form and posture. Today the traditional dry fly must compete with Thorax Duns and CDC Caddis Emergers for a place on the fly fisher's tippet.

Will the traditional dry fly eventually disappear along with the era that created it? I doubt it; at least I doubt that it will happen in my lifetime. For one thing, the traditional dry fly floats well on its hackles and hackle-fiber tails; for another, many tra-

ditional dry flies are versatile enough to perform a lot of varied duties; and finally, traditional dry flies still catch a lot of trout—these qualities should insure the traditional dry fly's continued popularity.

TYING DIFFICULTY
1 is easy; 5 is difficult

Pale Evening Dun	**3**
Ginger Quill	**3**
Dark Cahill	**4**

The Pale Evening Dun

The Pale Evening Dun artificial, predictably, imitates the mayfly commonly called the pale evening dun. Another common name for this mayfly, known to entomologists as *Ephemerella dorothea*, is the sulphur dun.

The pale-evening-dun hatch is important in the East. These little mayflies hatch from mid-May to early July, and the hatch shifts gradually from midday to twilight as the days warm into summer. Look for pale evening duns in swift runs and riffles. There is a western mayfly called a pale evening dun, but it's an entirely different insect than the one we focus on here.

Hackle-tip wings, like those on the Pale Evening Dun, are fairly common on traditional trout flies; you will also find them on the ubiquitous Adams. The best feathers that I have found for these wings are the hackles from a hen neck.

PALE EVENING DUN

HOOK: Standard dry fly, sizes 18 and 16 (the hook shown is a Daichii 1180).
THREAD: Yellow 8/0 or 6/0.
WINGS: Blue-dun hackle tips.
TAIL: Blue-dun hackle fibers.
BODY: Pale-yellow dubbing.
HACKLE: Blue-dun.

1. Pluck two hackles from a hen neck and hold them so their tips curve away from one another. Measure them against the hook, and then use the pinch to tie them in as wings, about three-quarters up the shank.

2. Snip the butts of the hen hackles at an angle and bind them under thread turns. Strip some hackle fibers, measure them, and use the pinch to tie them in as a tail.

3. Dub a tapered body to just past mid-shank. Draw the wings firmly up, and then back, and then trim away the fibers projecting forward from the wing's base. Crease the wings at their base with your thumb nail. (See "Wings--Upright Hackle Tip" in section X, "Basic Techniques.")

4. Add several tight thread turns against the front of the wings; this will set them upright. Measure, prepare, and tie in two hackles.

5. Wrap one hackle forward and secure its tip with two or three tight thread turns. Wind the second hackle through the first and secure its tip. Trim the tips and complete the fly as usual.

The Ginger Quill

When I was attending college in central Washington, I discovered the traditional Ginger Quill and found it consistently attractive to Yakima River rainbows. Such a pretty, delicate looking fly, and productive.

The stripped-peacock-quill body found on the Ginger Quill and other traditional dry flies is fragile. To toughen the quill, you can add a layer of head cement to the thread-covered shank before wrapping the quill, but I prefer to coat the quill after the fly is complete.

GINGER QUILL

HOOK: Standard dry fly, sizes 18 to 10 (the hook shown is a Mustad 94840).
THREAD: Tan or yellow 8/0 or 6/0.
WINGS: Duck quill.
TAIL: Ginger hackle fibers.
BODY: Stripped peacock quill.
HACKLE: Ginger hackles.

1. Snip a section from each of two matched duck quills. Hold the sections so that they curve away from each other, measure them, and tie them in three-quarters up the shank using the wing version of the pinch. The long sides of the sections should be down.

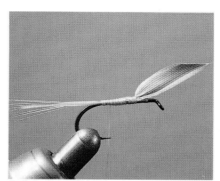

2. Snip the quill butts at an angle and bind them with thread. Strip a few fibers from a hackle, measure them, and tie them in using the pinch.

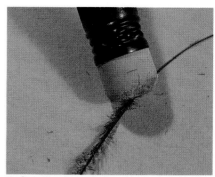

3. Strip the fibers from a peacock herl. This can be done with your fingernail or by rubbing the fibers off against a flat surface with an eraser.

4. Tie in the stripped quill and wrap it in consecutive turns to just past midshank to form a body. Secure the end of the quill with thread turns, and then trim off the quill's end.

5. Set the wings upright as described in section X, "Basic Techniques" under "Wings—Upright Quill." Prepare, size, and then tie in two hackles. Wrap one hackle and secure its tip with two or three tight thread turns. Wind the second hackle through the first and secure its tip. Trim the tips and complete the fly as usual.

6. Here is a Ginger Quill tied more sparsely than the one shown at the beginning of this section; you can tie traditional dry flies even more sparsely than this if you like. Note the lacquered quill body.

The Cahills

To me, the Dark Cahill and Light Cahill represent the ideal of the traditional dry fly. Their soft, muskrat- or badger-fur bodies, the subtle contrast of their hackles and tails against those bodies, and their gracefully curved, finely marked wood-duck wings all tell of elegance. These characteristics also make the Cahills a fine choice for imitating mayflies from dark to light, and for imitating other insects.

Wood duck is currently scarce and quite expensive; mallard feathers dyed wood-duck color make a good substi-tute. You may find wood-duck wings a bit tricky to handle; the trick is to measure carefully, master the wing variation of the pinch, and handle the fibers firmly and deliberately. The leftover tips of wood-duck feathers also make good wings.

The Light Cahill and Dark Cahill were created on the East Coast by Dan Cahill, but are now in use across America.

DARK CAHILL

HOOK: Standard dry fly, sizes 20 to 10 (the hook shown is a Partridge L3A).
THREAD: Tan, brown, or black 8/0 or 6/0.
WINGS: Wood duck or dyed mallard.
TAIL: Brown hackle fibers.
BODY: Muskrat fur.
HACKLE: Brown.

LIGHT CAHILL

HOOK: Standard dry fly, sizes 20 to 10 (the hook shown is a Partridge L3A).
THREAD: Tan or cream 8/0 or 6/0.
WINGS: Wood duck or dyed mallard.
TAIL: Ginger hackle fibers.
BODY: Cream badger underfur.
HACKLE: Ginger.

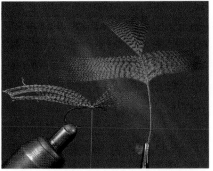

1. Strip the fuzz from the base of a wood-duck feather, and then strip a section from each side of the feather. Set the sections back to back, measure them against the hook, and tie them in about three-quarters up the shank using the wing version of the pinch. Each section should be at least as wide as the hook's gape, even as wide as the shank is long.

2. Trim the butts of the wood duck at an angle and then bind them with thread turns. Strip some hackle fibers, measure them against the hook, and then use the pinch to tie them in as a tail. Trim the tail's butts and bind them with thread.

3. Snip some muskrat fur from the hide, and with it dub a tapered body to just past mid-shank.

4. Pull the wings firmly upright, add tight thread turns against the front of the fibers, divide the wings, set each wing upright with thread (see "Wings—Wood Duck" in section X, "Basic Techniques").

5. Size, prepare, and tie in two hackles. Wrap the hackles one at a time to just behind the eye; secure each hackle with two or three thread turns. Trim the hackle tips; build and complete a thread head.

VII

ROUGH-WATER FLIES

Introduction To Rough-Water Flies

Before discussing the properties of rough-water flies, it's important to consider the angler's part in keeping flies afloat. Any fly will float its longest and highest if these simple guidelines are followed:

1. Apply floatant to the leader as well as to the fly, and discard floating fly lines that tend to sink easily and replace them with new ones—if your leader, line, or both sink, they will surely draw your fly down. Forget the theory about how sunk leaders are least conspicuous—the fish won't have time to inspect, and you won't have a floating fly if your leader is down in churning currents.

2. Apply floatant thoroughly but modestly to a dry fly—flies untreated with floatant sink too easily; flies drenched in floatant do the same.

3. Try to set your fly gently atop the water—slapping down a dry fly starts it on its ride already half sunk, and your objective is already half lost.

4. Unless you want to deliberately twitch or skitter your dry fly, avoid drag judiciously—"drag," the effect of current pulling at a fly through a taught leader, line, or both, will often yank a dry fly under. Slack-line and slack-leader casts, adequate tippet length, and skillful line handling will all greatly reduce the risk of drag.

For years I battled the idea that heavy hackling was the best way to keep a dry fly atop rough water. I tried sponge bodies, buoyant extended bodies, and everything else I could think of to replace the bush of hackle fibers. I haven't given up yet, but I have to admit that a thick hackle collar remains the first part of the rough-water solution; I almost always use three hackles for my rough-water hackle collars (except, of course, when I am using long saddle hackles, exceptional neck hackles, or tying parachute hackles). After the hackle come the wings and tail—if these are buoyant, that helps too. Finally, to some degree the body thickness and material can offer buoyancy—this is especially true of the Humpy with its hump of air-pocketed hair over its back.

Parachute-hackled flies are usually my choice on water that is well broken but not truly rough (see "The Parabright"); truly rough calls for true rough-water flies. Other rough-water flies found in other sections of this book include the Goddard Caddis and Poly Humpy.

TYING DIFFICULTY
1 is easy; 5 is difficult

Blonde Wulff	3
H and L Variant	4
Humpy	5
Rat-Faced McDougal	5

The Blonde Wulff

Even among the giants of fly fishing—those whose influence on our sport is legend—there is a special place for Lee Wulff. Lee is now gone, but his Wulff series of fly patterns is his legacy.

The Wulff flies run from pale, such as the Blonde Wulff, to dark, such as the Gray Wulff. This gives the angler a full range of hues from a single fly style. By also varying size, the angler can create a solid base of fast-water dry flies. The Wulff series is not only effective for trout but also for Atlantic salmon and steelhead.

BLONDE WULFF

HOOK: Standard dry fly, sizes 16 to 6 (the hook shown is an Eagle Claw #D59).
THREAD: Tan or black (I've seen both listed) 8/0 or 6/0; but I prefer to at least start with 3/0 so I can really secure the hair wings and tails.
WINGS: Light tan deer hair or bleached elk (elk is shown). (Lee intended the Wulffs to be flexible patterns, so tan calf tail, tan buck tail, or any reasonable substitute is fine.)
TAIL: Light-tan deer hair, bleached elk, or substitute.
BODY: Tan dubbing (or yarn).
HACKLE: Ginger (note that I substituted barred ginger; note also the effect).

1. Comb, stack, measure, and use the pinch to tie in a bunch of elk hair for wings. Trim the butts of the hair at an angle, and bind them with thread turns.

2. Comb, stack, measure, and use the pinch to tie in another bunch of elk hair as a tail. Trim the butts of the tail at an angle to splice with the butts of the wings. Cover the butts of wings and tail with thread.

3. If you started with 3/0 thread, you can switch to 8/0 or 6/0 now. Dub a tapered body no further than midshank. Divide and set the wings upright as described in section X, "Basic Techniques" under "Wings—Upright Hair." Size, prepare, and tie in three (or two) hackles.

4. Wind the first hackle and secure its tip with tight thread turns; wind the second hackle through this first one and secure its tip; do the same with the third hackle (if you chose to use three). Trim the hackles' tips and complete the fly with a thread head as usual.

The H and L Variant

The H and L Variant is an old-timer among rough-water dry flies. It has wings and a tail of calf tail. The method most tiers use for the body is to partially strip a peacock quill; when wrapped, the bare quill forms the rear half of the body and the fiber-covered quill the front half. This allows you to create both the front and rear body sections in one step, and a thin layer of head cement over the thread-wrapped shank will help toughen the body. I prefer to tie in both halves of the body separately as shown—with a bit of head cement on the bare quill, this body is tough indeed. The H and L Variant is sometimes tied with over-size hackles, in traditional variant fashion, and it is sometimes tied with hackles of conventional size; I prefer the conventional. The H and L Variant is also referred to as the House and Lot.

H AND L VARIANT

HOOK: Standard dry fly, sizes 16 to 10 (the hook shown is a Dai-Riki 305).
THREAD: Black 3/0 first, then 8/0 or 6/0.
WINGS: White calf tail.
TAIL: White calf tail.
BODY: Rear half: stripped peacock herl; front half: peacock herl.
HACKLE: Furnace (brown is fine).

1. To best secure the wings and tail, begin with 3/0 thread. Comb, stack, measure, and then use the pinch to tie in the wing hair. Trim the hair's butts at an angle and bind them with thread.

2. Comb, stack, measure, and use the pinch to tie in the tail hair. Snip the butts at an angle and bind them with thread. If you started with 3/0 thread, you can switch now to 8/0 or 6/0. Strip a peacock quill, tie it in, and wrap it up one-quarter of the shank. Secure the quill with thread; trim the quill.

3. Tie in a peacock quill (unstripped) near its tip, spin the quill and thread together (see "Reinforcing Peacock Herl" in section X, "Basic Techniques"), and wrap this thread-quill rope up one-quarter of the shank. Secure the end of the quill under thread turns and trim the quill.

4. Set the wings upright (see "Wings—Upright Hair" in section X, "Basic Techniques"). Tie in three hackles (two is acceptable, but I prefer three, especially for hook sizes 12 and larger). One by one, wind each hackle, secure its tip with thread turns, and trim its tip.

5. Build and whip finish a thread head. With the sharp point of a round toothpick (or similar object) add head cement to the quill body and the thread head.

The Humpy

The Humpy seems to have established itself as the number-one rough-water dry fly. Its hair hump adds buoyancy, and the tips of the fibers that form this hump make the wings. Clever. I will show you a few unconventional techniques for tying this fly that make it quick to tie and durable.

In *The Second Fly Tyer's Almanac*, Kathy Buckner gives an excellent description-demonstration of tying the Humpy. She states that "The key to the whole thing is the length of the tail," and says that "If the tail is the right length, everything else will come out right." That's true, because all the critical measurements come from the tail.

Here are a few pointers for tying the Humpy that I have discovered on my own: Elk hair is best for the humpy's hump and wings—elk hair is generally much tougher than deer, and the hump is secured at both ends

which makes it vulnerable between. Determine the thickness of the hump-wing hair bunch to suit the wings; don't worry about the hump. Again, careful measuring of the tail and wing-hump hair is critical (see "Measuring" in section X, "Basic Techniques"), but even when measuring is done carefully, variations in hook design will vary the length of the wings somewhat, though not to any real consequence. Single-strand floss used as thread for the first few steps will make the Humpy go quickly—the floss covers the hair much faster than would any thread, and the floss's strength allows you to really secure the hair. When drawing the hump-wing hair up and forward, stroke your grasp up the hairs to even out tension among them.

I have developed my own style for tying the Humpy, but that style was formed from Kathy's insight.

HUMPY

HOOK: Standard dry fly, sizes 18 to 10 (the hook shown is a Tiemco 101).
THREAD: Single-strand floss and 8/0, 6/0 or 3/0 thread (both floss and thread should be the same color; colors include yellow, red, black, orange, green, and fluorescent versions of these colors).
TAIL: Moose-body hairs.
HUMP, AND WINGS: Natural elk hair.
HACKLE: One grizzly and one brown.

1. With single-strand floss in a floss bobbin, start the floss at midshank; start the floss just as you would thread. (Or, of course, you can just use thread in a thread bobbin.) Comb, stack, measure *carefully*, and tie in a bunch of moose-body hair at the bend for a tail using the pinch—the tail should be *exactly* one full hook's length (see "Measuring" in section X "Basic Techniques"). Trim the tails' butts.

2. Wrap the floss to just short of midshank. Comb and stack a bunch of elk hair. Measure the stacked elk by setting its tips directly above the tips of the tail—all tips should end at *exactly* the same point. Trim the elk's butts *directly* over the tip of the eye.

3. Set the cut edge of the elk at *exactly* midshank and use the pinch to tie it in with tight turns of floss. Lift the butts slightly as you wrap the floss down the elk to the bend and then back to midshank.

4. Lift the elk up and then forward and down over the body under firm tension. Hold the elk firmly as you work two turns of floss over it and pull them tight. Add a few more turns of floss and then switch to the trout thread (no need to switch if you are already using thread).

5. Work the thread forward slightly over the elk to provide space for hackling. Divide and set the elk-hair tips upright as wings.

6. Prepare and size two hackles and tie them in. Wind the first hackle (either the grizzly or the brown, makes no difference) to the eye and secure its tip with three tight turns of thread; do the same with the second hackle. Trim the hackles' tips and complete the fly as usual. You can use three hackles, as I've suggested for the other rough-water flies, but the hair hump adds enough buoyancy that I find two hackles sufficient.

The Rat-Faced McDougal

Harry and Elsie Darby, the famous fly tiers of Roscoe, New York, made popular this fly that Harry said was created at his request by "Percy Jennings, an amateur fly tier from Cold Spring Harbor, known among anglers for the time he caught a 3 1/2-pound brown on a backcast." The Rat-Faced McDougal was originally tied with grizzly-hackle-tip wings, but Harry wrote in his book *Catskill Flytier* that white calf-tail wings were "more visible, just as effective." He never mentioned the fly's tail, but I would be tempted to use white or tan calf tail for it, though I've stuck with Harry's ginger hackle fibers here.

RAT-FACED McDOUGAL

HOOK: Standard dry fly, sizes 16 to 10 (the hook shown is a Gamakatsu F 13).
THREAD: White 8/0 or 6/0 (I prefer 3/0 because it really secures the hair wing); for the spun-hair body, gray size-A rod-winding thread.
TAIL: Ginger hackle fibers.
BODY: Spun and shaped deer or caribou hair.
WINGS: White calf tail.
HACKLE: Ginger.

1. Start the trout-size thread right at the bend; use just enough tight turns to really secure the thread. Strip, measure, and use the pinch to tie in a bunch of hackle fibers for a tail, and then trim the fiber's butts—keep the tail wraps short. (Note that we are not tying in the wing first as usual; this is typical with spun-hair-bodied dry flies.)

2. Switch to the size-A thread. Snip a bunch of deer or caribou hair from the hide and comb it (shown is caribou). Snip the butts of the hair square and neat.

3. Work the bunch down around the shank. The squared butts should extend back slightly from the bend and cover the thread wraps. Take two turns of thread over the hair and hold the hair in place as you draw the turns tight. If all this is done with modest care, you won't have to shape this part of the body later.

4. Comb, spin, and compress bunches of hair to about midshank (a total of two to four). Whip finish and trim the thread.

5. Trim the hair to a tapered body. (See "Shaping Spun Hair" in section X," Basic Techniques.")

6. Start the trout thread again. Comb, stack, and then measure a bunch of calf tail; snip its butts to a length that will put them right up against the body. Tie in the calf tail using the reverse pinch. Cover the calf tail's butts with tight thread turns. Divide the hair into two wings and set them upright.

7. Size, prepare, and tie in two or three hackles. Wind the first hackle forward in spaced turns to the eye and secure the tip with three tight thread turns; do the same with the second hackle and finally (if there is one) the third. Trim the hackles' tips and finish the fly as usual. (Refer to section X, "Basic Techniques" for help on any of these steps.)

VIII

TINY FLIES

Introduction To Tiny Flies

The term "midge" has two meanings to the fly fisher: first, an insect, of the family *Chironomidae* (which resembles a mosquito and is among the smallest of trout-food insects) and second, any tiny dry fly. The inconsistencies can be confusing—if you tie a midge to your tippet to fish a hatch of midges, that makes sense, but does it make sense to tie on a midge for a hatch of mayflies? And no one seems certain whether or not tiny artificial nymphs are midges. Now you see why I like to call tiny flies, tiny flies. But be prepared, as "midge" is an accepted and oft-used term among fly fishers.

Chironomids

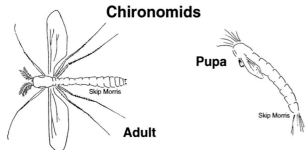

Tiny flies are today a solid part of fly fishing. Where once the single-minded feeding of trout on minuscule mayflies, midges, or caddisflies meant that it was time to break for lunch—or even quit for the day—many anglers now consider this a time of exacting and exciting sport.

The practical matter of getting a hook firmly embedded into a trout's mouth becomes more complicated when that hook is tiny. Vince Marinaro advised bending the point slightly to one side to widen the gape—I've tried it, it helps. Ring-eye hooks are popular for tiny flies; I'm still experimenting in this area. In *The Versatile Fly Tyer*, Dick Talleur points out that quality hackles have stiff, dense fibers that can impede the penetration of tiny hooks. To cure this he started "trimming Vs out of the bottom" of his tiny-fly hackle collars. Finally, the points of your tiny hooks *must* be sharp.

It is to the benefit of the tier that tiny flies allow less inspection from trout than do larger flies and therefore can be, and usually are, simple in design and construction.

Here are a few general points regarding the tying of tiny flies that will help make this a pleasant task. First, a vise with fine jaws (many vises can accept several jaws) offers good tying access on tiny hooks. Second, scale down your materials in both size and quantity—use short-fibered peacock herl for tiny flies, and add only three to (at most) eight turns of hackle to a dry fly of size 20 or smaller, and use almost no dubbing at all. Third, consider some kind of magnifier (see "Magnifier" in section XIII,"Dry-Fly Tools") as this can make tying tiny much easier and more pleasant, even for those with good eyesight. Fourth, although there are special threads for tying tiny, the best I have found for tiny flies, providing you use as few turns of it as possible, is 8/0. Finally, although special tools are made for tying tiny flies, I've never found much value in them beyond the matter of vise jaws, though some tiers like tiny tools for tiny flies. My point is that tiny tools are optional, so you can start tying tiny with the tools you have.

TYING DIFFICULTY
1 is easy; 5 is difficult

(Because the size of these flies increases the challenge of tying them, all move one degree up in difficulty over what they would be in moderate size)

Griffith's Gnat	3
Antron Caddis	3
Trico Poly Wing Spinner	3
Adams	4

The Griffith's Gnat

Midges are tiny, but they are often a big part of a trout's diet. Because midges often hatch in huge numbers and are quite helpless, some heavy trout will come up to them.

The Griffith's Gnat imitates a half-hatched midge. To suggest this incomplete metamorphosis, the Griffith's Gnat is usually fished awash, half-sunk and half-floating, in the surface. Because midges have the unwholesome habit of gathering into clumps as they mate atop the water, a large Griffith's Gnat, size 14 or 12, can be used to suggest this lustful tangle of legs, bodies, and wings.

George Griffith, who helped start Trout Unlimited, created the Griffith's Gnat. If trout are rising steadily and gently along smooth glides at twilight, give me a size 24 Griffith's Gnat and I'll expect to turn a few fish.

GRIFFITH'S GNAT

HOOK: Midge or standard dry fly, sizes 24 to 12 (the hook shown is an Orvis 1637).
THREAD: Olive or black 8/0.
HACKLE: Grizzly.
BODY: Peacock herl.

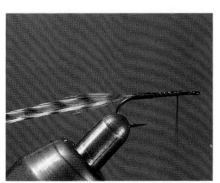

1. Start the thread and, at the bend, tie in a hackle that has been sized and prepared.

2. Tie in a short-fibered peacock herl at the bend. Trim the herl's end and work the thread to just behind the eye. Wrap the herl forward in consecutive turns and secure its end with three thread turns. Wrap the herl with only modest tension—fine herl is especially fragile.

3. Trim the herl's end, and then palmer the hackle up the body in four to six turns. Secure the hackle's tip with thread turns, trim the hackle's tip, and complete the fly with a thread head as usual.

The Antron Caddis

In my introduction for this section I mentioned that tiny and simple go hand in hand when it comes to fly tying—as you can see by the photograph above, one would be hard pressed to find a better example of this than the Antron Caddis. Actually, this fly is often fished in larger sizes, but I think it is especially good tiny. I discovered the Antron Caddis in *Fly Patterns of Yellowstone* by Craig Mathews and John Juracek.

The best deer hair for the wing is fine but spongy—the sponginess helps the wing to flare.

The Antron Caddis is generally a smooth-water fly.

ANTRON CADDIS

> *HOOK*: Midge or standard dry fly, sizes 22 to 14 (the hook shown is a Partridge L4A).
> *THREAD*: Olive or brown 8/0 or 6/0.
> *ABDOMEN*: Green, olive, black, or brown antron dubbing.
> *WING*: Light or dark deer hair.
> *THORAX*: Tan or brown hare's mask or Australian opossum.

1. Dub a body of antron two-thirds up the hook's shank.

2. Comb, stack, measure, and use the pinch to tie in a bunch of deer hair as a wing; the wing should extend to the very rear of the hook, or slightly beyond. Use tight thread turns to flare the wing. Cut the wing's butts before mounting the wing or trim the butts at an angle after the wing is secured.

3. Dub the thorax a bit roughly with hare's mask or Australian opossum. Complete the thread head as usual. Pick out a few hairs from the sides of the thorax to suggest legs.

The Trico Poly Wing Spinner

Beginning each year in mid to late summer, many slow-moving trout streams across America play host to huge hatching-mating movements of tiny *Tricorythodes*, a mayfly of various species, some of which are so small that imitations must be tied on size 28 hooks. That "tricos," as they are nicknamed, are unusually tiny is appropriate, because everything about them is unusual—the male trico's tails are outlandishly long, tricos have no hind wings like most mayflies, and the wings they do have are, of all things, whitish—whitish!

Tricos hatch in the morning or around midday. Sometimes the dun is important, in which case any mayfly dun pattern with dark-brown body and light hackle, light tail and, if you want them, wings, will do fine. But I usually find a preponderance of spinners, and these I imitate with the Trico Polly Wing Spinner.

TRICO POLY WING SPINNER

HOOK: Midge or standard dry fly, sizes 26 to 20 (shown is a Dai-Riki 310).
THREAD: Brown 8/0.
TAIL: White or ginger hackle fibers.
ABDOMEN: Olive dubbing.
WINGS: White poly yarn.
THORAX: Brown dubbing.

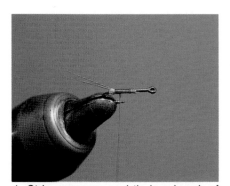

1. Strip, measure, and tie in a bunch of hackle fibers as a split tail. (This pattern imitates the female trico, so tails should be of standard length.)

2. Dub a tapered abdomen up two-thirds of the shank. Using the pinch, tie in a bunch of poly yarn. Pull the yarn out to the sides of the thorax and crisscross the thread around the yarn at its tie-in point.

3. Add more crisscrossed thread turns around the wings' base with brown-dubbed thread. Add some dubbing in front of the wing, and create a thread head.

4. Raise and trim the wings as one. Add head cement.

The Adams and the Adams Midge

Virtually every experienced fly fisher in America must either have fished or have heard of the Adams. A few years ago the Adams was often described by writers as the most popular dry fly in America. Today it may not be, but popular it remains.

The first Adamses I saw were tied on tiny hooks. "A good imitation of the blue winged olive," the fly-shop salesman said. He was right—a tiny Adams was and is effective during this mayfly hatch. But the somber, natural appearance of the Adams makes it a good imitation of many mayflies and even some caddisflies, especially active, buzzing caddisflies. So the Adams is useful under lots of conditions and in a range of sizes from tiny to large. Still, I like it best tiny.

The Adams Midge seems to be a response to the notion that tiny and simple go hand in hand—the wings are omitted. Since that's the only significant difference between the Adams and Adams Midge, I couldn't see any point in listing both patterns. On the Adams, the traditional hackle-fiber tail is sometimes replaced now with a tail of moose-body hairs. Hen neck hackle makes the best Adams wings I have found. The Adams shown is tied sparsely in typical tiny-fly style.

The Adams was created by Leonard Halladay.

ADAMS

HOOK: Standard dry fly, sizes 20 to 10 for the Adams, 24 to 20 for the Adams Midge (the hook shown is a Mustad 94859).
THREAD: Gray or black.
WINGS: Grizzly hackle tips (omitted on the Adams Midge).
TAIL: Grizzly and brown hackle fibers mixed (or moose-body hair).
BODY: Muskrat fur.
HACKLE: Brown and grizzly mixed.

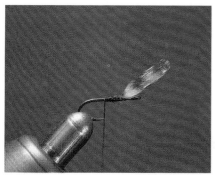

1. Measure and tie in the hackle wings using the pinch—don't strip or even trim the hackles beforehand (see "Wings—Upright Hackle Tip" in section X, "Basic Techniques"). Snip the wings' butts and bind them with thread.

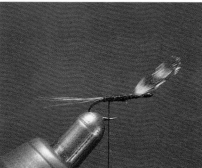

2. Strip a small bunch of brown hackle fibers, measure them, and, using the pinch, tie them in to begin the tail. Atop those, tie in some grizzly fibers, then more brown. Trim the tail's butts and bind them with thread.

3. Dub a tapered body to just past mid-shank. Draw back the wings, trim the fibers at their base, and set the wings upright with turns of thread.

4. Size, prepare, and tie in one brown hackle and one grizzly. Wind one hackle to just behind the eye in two to four turns (remember, tiny flies require little hackle), and then secure it with tight thread turns. Do the same with the other hackle. Trim the hackles' tips. Complete the fly with the usual thread head.

IX

HIGHLY VISIBLE FLIES

Introduction To Highly Visible Flies

Conditions that call for highly visible flies are many: low light, long casts, rough water, tiny flies, imperfect eyesight, and even vacation-induced laziness.

After repeated testing with my fishing partners, our hands-down favorite highly visible color is light, bright yellow. Oranges and chartreuses are good, but no match. I also feel that a light color is least noticeable to trout, because they see a dry fly against a light sky, thus a light color is less apparent than a dark or even moderately dark one. Even at twilight the sky is light—look up the next time the river is all but lost in blackness and you'll be surprised. I have had keen anglers tell me they are convinced that an unnatural wing color does not concern trout, but seeing my fly does concern me.

In all but the lowest-light conditions (nearly night), polarized sun glasses dramatically improve your ability to see a dry fly, especially one with bright colors.

You will see several methods here for adding bright yarn to flies. In situations where trout are choosy—spring creeks, lakes, low water—I add only as much bright color as needed, unless of course the insect I am imitating has bright colors as in the case of the huge, yellow *Hexegenia* mayfly. In broken water, trout have no opportunity to inspect a fly closely, so I use lots of bright yarn.

There are times when seeing your fly is impossible no matter what you do. In such situations, I have had good results by estimating the place where my fly should be and striking when a trout rises there; perhaps two out of three times I'm wrong, but that one out of three is a fine payoff.

Keen anglers consistently take difficult trout on bright-winged dry flies. At fly-tying clinics I am often asked why a trout would overlook such an inconsistency as a bright-yellow wing when the natural has a wing of slate gray. That's when I share my duck theory, and here it is: If I see a duck floating on a pond, I will instantly identify the duck by its flat bill and overall form; the last and least likely manner in which I will identify the duck is by peering underwater to find its webbed feet. Of course if the duck is walking on land I will notice its distinctive webbed feet

immediately; that is because the duck's feet are now in my world—the world of air. Trout also focus on whatever is in their world—the world of water. So when a trout sees a Matt's Adult Stone floating overhead, it notices the orange bulk and gray orb that press through the surface and the pointed stubs that push down; that's how a trout sees a Matt's Adult Stone. Of least importance to the trout are the hair wing and collar hairs in the world of air.

Imagine that you see someone peering around underwater and you ask, "Why are you looking under that duck?"

"Is it a duck? truly? I couldn't tell, I haven't seen any webbed feet."

"What about its bill?, the shape of its head?—its quacking? It's obviously a duck."

"Well, I haven't gotten to those yet; I have to find its feet first." If this feet-first approach to duck identification makes sense to you, then you will probably believe, no matter what anyone says, that trout focus on wings in order to identify floating insects.

I'm not suggesting that wings are of no consequence; it is likely that cautious trout pay some attention to wings and other features above the water's surface. What I *am* suggesting is that surface features get the least scrutiny and that the presence or absence of wings is probably all that the trout will notice; a bit of yellow should be of no consequence.

TYING DIFFICULTY
1 is easy; 5 is difficult

A General Approach

The visibility of practically any conventional dry fly can be enhanced. The trick is to get bright poly yarn into the fly in such a way that the yarn is visible to you but obscured from the trout. This is easily accomplished because a trout views a dry fly from below while you view it from above. The following examples demonstrate.

Flies With A Swept Wing

This category includes any dry fly with wings sweeping back over its body. Of the flies we have explored thus far, a few examples of such a wing include the Elk Hair Caddis, Clark's Stonefly, and Letort Hopper; caddis, stonefly, and hopper imitations often fall into this category. With these flies, a tuft of yarn tied in over the original wing is apparent to angler, obscured from trout. (The hook shown is a Gamakatsu F13.)

1. Here, the Elk Hair Caddis is used as an example. The wing was already tied in, and the yarn was added atop it. Two snips and the yarn is trimmed. With other patterns the wing and yarn may be added earlier in the tying sequence, but the general rule is this: The swept wing is added, and the yarn is tied in next.

2. A finished highly visible Elk Hair Caddis.

Flies With Upright Wings

This includes all sorts of dry flies, especially those that imitate mayflies. Examples of dry flies with an upright wing that we have explored thus far include the Dark Green Drake and H and L Variant. Hiding bright poly yarn from trout in an upright wing is difficult, but the yarn can be blended into the wing. Besides, it is the parts of a fly that are on or under the water's surface that trout see best and concentrate on most. (The hooks shown are Orvis 1523.)

1. Here is a Dark Green Drake with the bright yarn added before the regular dark-yarn wing. When the wing is tipped up, the bright yarn will lead the rest of the wing. To make the bright yarn trail the wing, simply tie in the bright yarn after the dark.

2. A finished highly visible Dark Green Drake

3. Here is an H and L Variant with its calf-tail wings set upright. Push the wings apart. Fold the yarn around the thread, pinch both ends of the yarn together, and slide the yarn down the thread to a place between the wings. Take a turn or two of thread to secure the yarn's position.

4. Add crisscrossed thread turns to position the yarn with its ends projecting out to the sides. Wrap the thread around each wing base and the yarn.

5. Draw the yarn tips back from the wings and trim both ends of the yarn with a single snip. The yarn can be shorter than the wings, longer than the wings, or equal to the wings—whichever you deem appropriate. Add hackles and complete the fly as usual.

6. A finished highly visible H and L Variant.

1. On this Speckled Poly Wing Spinner, a section of bright poly yarn has been tied onto the top of the thorax in line with the shank. The wings are tied in first; then the bright yarn is added just behind them. Dubbing is worked all around the wings and bright yarn; then the wings are pulled down to trim, and the tuft is pulled up to trim. (You can add the bright poly yarn to the Poly Wing Spinner's poly-yarn wings, but since the wings are right on the water, the bright yarn will be apparent to the fish.)

2. A finished highly visible Speckled Poly Wing Spinner.

Flies With Spent Wings Or None

Flies of this sort that we have tied include the following: Poly Wing Spinner, Black Flying Ant, Black Ant, and Foam Beetle. The yarn can't be easily blended with the wings here, especially in those flies with no wings, so a small tuft of yarn is set above the body. Simply tie in the yarn in whatever manner is easiest.
(The hook shown is a Dai-Riki 305.)

Replacing Wings

Another approach is to entirely replace all wings with bright poly yarn. This asks a bit of accommodation from the trout, but some anglers do well with flies that have entirely bright wings, and some of the trout that take these flies are experienced and cautious. The bright wing most visible to the angler is surely the upright, unobscured wing on a parachute fly.

The Poly Humpy

I thought I had a fine idea when I used poly yarn for the hump and wings of a Humpy; to be sure, it *was* a fine idea, but it wasn't my own. One day I was reading an old issue of *Fly Tyer* magazine and found the source of my great idea: Under the title "Variations on the Poly Scene," fly tier R. Monty Montplaisir described how to tie a Humpy with a poly-yarn wing and hump.

The Poly Humpy has a lot to recommend it over the original Humpy; the Poly Humpy is the easiest to tie, floats longest, and is the more durable. The Poly Humpy's greatest benefit may be the high visibility it offers if its yarn is bright.

Yarn wings are fluffy, so it will help you neatly add hackle later if you can firmly compress the wings at their base; the best way to do this is to make tight wraps around the wings' bases. If you need more help with the Poly Humpy refer back to the original Humpy in section VII, "Rough-Water Flies."

POLY HUMPY

HOOK: Standard dry fly. Monty suggests sizes 20 to 8, but my smallest is 18. (The hook shown is a Gamakatsu F-31.)
THREAD: Red or yellow single-strand floss, followed by 8/0 or 6/0 in the floss's color.
TAIL: Moose-body hair.
BODY: Tying thread over the yarn.
WINGS AND HUMP: Monty suggests tan poly yarn, which is fine, but for a highly visible fly use a bright color.
HACKLE: One grizzly, one brown.

1. Using single-strand floss as thread (or just use thread), comb, stack, and measure a bunch of moose-body hair and tie it in as a tail. Trim the tail's butts.

2. At midshank, tie in the poly yarn and wrap the floss down it to the bend. Wrap the floss back up to midshank and make sure the floss covers the poly yarn completely. Trim the yarn's butt.

3. Pull the yarn up and then forward and down over the top of the floss body. Secure the yarn with a few tight turns of floss. Switch to regular tying thread.

4. Crease the end of the yarn upright, and then split the yarn and divide it into two wings. Set the wings into position with thread as usual (see "Wings—Upright Hair" in section X, "Basic Techniques").

5. Size, prepare, and tie in the two hackles. Wrap one hackle to the head area and secure its tip with tight thread turns. Wind the second hackle forward through the first and secure its tip. Trim the hackles' tips and complete the thread head.

6. Pull the yarn wings up together and, with a single snip, trim them to wing length. Add cement to the thread head.

The Parabright

So far as I know, this particular combination of materials and colors is mine, unique. But it must be added that many bright-winged parachute flies have come from other vises—Al Troth has been working with bright-winged parachute flies for some time. The Parabright in both its light and dark versions is fast becoming my first choice for broken water, short of the kind of turbulence that requires true rough-water flies.

PARABRIGHT LIGHT

HOOK: Standard dry fly, sizes 18 to 10 (the hook shown is
            an Orvis 1523).
THREAD: Tan 8/0 or 6/0.
WING: Bright-yellow poly yarn.
HACKLE: Ginger.
TAIL: Tan calf tail.
BODY: Tan poly dubbing.

PARABRIGHT DARK

HOOK: Standard dry fly, sizes 18 to 10.
THREAD: Brown 8/0 or 6/0.
WING: Bright-yellow poly yarn.
HACKLE: Brown.
TAIL: Brown calf tail.
BODY: Brown poly dubbing.

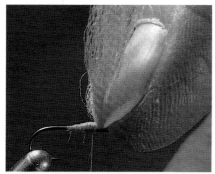

1. Using the pinch, tie in a bunch of poly yarn about three-quarters up the shank. Snip the butts of the yarn at an angle and cover the cut ends with thread. Crease the yarn upright with your thumbnail. (As an alternate, use the second yarn-wing method described under "The Dark Green Drake.")

2. Wind a light layer of thread up and another then back down the base of the yarn wing. Set the wing securely with thread (see "Parachute Hackles" in section XI, "Hackle— Still the Standard"). Prepare and then tie in a hackle against the wing base by wrapping a layer of thread up its stem and the wing's base and then wrapping another layer back down.

3. Draw the hackle's stem back along the shank and secure it with thread wraps. Comb, stack, measure, and then tie in a bunch of calf tail at the bend for a tail. Trim the butts of the calf and bind them with thread. Dub a tapered body to just in front of the wing.

4. Wind the hackle in consecutive turns down the wing's base to the body; use plenty of turns if this fly is meant for broken water. Secure the hackle's tip with three tight thread turns.

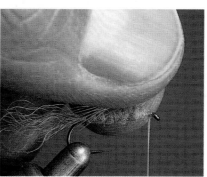

5. Draw the hackles back from the eye, build a thread head, and then release the hackles and slip a whip finish over the thread head. Add head cement as usual.

6. When the head cement is hard, trim the wing to length, and then tug the wing and hackle straight. You can trim the wing to a point if you wish, which gives you less wing to see, but may help the fly land upright.

X

BASIC TECHNIQUES

Breaking The Thread's End

This technique was shown to me by Dan Byford, creator of a popular, deadly fly called the Zonker. When you first start the thread, make a few turns in one place, pull the end of the thread sharply forward, and the thread will break against the hook. This saves time because you won't have to bother with scissors. But remember, you must pull the thread-end *forward*.

Pull the thread end sharply forward (for clarity, fly-line backing is shown).

Broken Thread

Every tier accidentally breaks thread. Here is the best solution I have found: Clamp hackle pliers to the remaining end of the thread, let the pliers hang, pull more thread from the bobbin, start the thread anew, wrap the new thread back over the end of the old, trim both the new and old thread ends, and continue tying.

With hackle pliers hanging from the broken thread end, start the thread anew over the last turns of the broken thread, and then trim both the new and old thread ends.

Bullet Head

For most tiers, a bullet head is easier to create than a spun-hair head. The bullet head is the least durable of the two, but if tied with elk hair rather than deer, it will hold up well.

You can either slip the butts of the hair straight into and around the hook's eye (especially good with ring-eye hooks), or you can hold the butts atop the shank, take light thread turns around them, and then work the butts down around the shank. Tighten the turns, and then bind the hair butts. To form the head, push your fingertip straight into the eye to spread the hair, work the hair back with your thumb and fingers, or use a drinking straw as shown (a method developed by my friend Rod Robbinson). The length of the collar hairs is largely a matter of style, but my formula is to trim the hair so that it reaches from the tip of the eye to the bend (the end of the body if an extended body is used); I then tie in the hair about 1/8" up from its cut ends. Once the head is formed, a thread collar is added and whip finished; head cement is added to the thread collar only.

1. Comb, stack, measure, and trim the butts of a bunch of elk hair. with the thread just behind the eye, work the hair butts around the shank and take two thread turns around them.

2. Pull the thread tight, bind the butts, work the thread back, and then push your finger straight into the hair to the eye, flaring hair.

3. Stroke the hair back or push a drinking straw back over the eye as shown. Work two turns of thread over the hair, and then pull the thread tight.

Dubbing

The common, simplest approach to dubbing is described in section I, "Essential Techniques." Shown here are two alternate methods. First is a method that results in tightly wound fibers and a slim body.

1. Lay dubbing fibers in the palm of your hand and tease them into a roughly triangular shape.

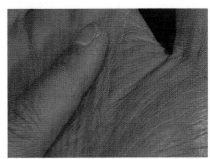

2. Slide a finger across your palm a few times to roll the fibers into a tapered rope, and then trim the rope's very tip to eliminate fuzz.

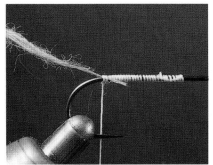

3. Using the pinch (or a light turn), secure the fine tip of the rope under a turn or two of thread.

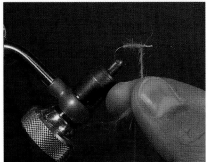

4. Spin the thread and large end of the rope together, and then hold the end of the rope-thread combination as you wind it up the shank.

This second dubbing method—the dubbing loop—can create a scruffy effect, a bulky one, or a trim, tight one, all depending on how you handle it. The benefits of a dubbing loop are that it secures the dubbing especially well and that it allows for quick bulk and a rough-but-secure effect. The loop is formed by pulling some extra thread off the bobbin, looping it over a dubbing twister (or even your finger), and then wrapping the thread around the shank again and wrapping back far enough to lock in both ends of the loop. For the scruffy effect, hook a dubbing twister (or simply a half-straightened paper clip) onto the loop, distribute fur inside the loop, twist the loop, and wrap the thread-fur combination up the shank.

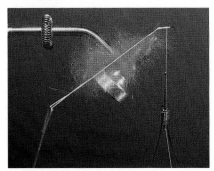

1. Distribute the fur inside the loop.

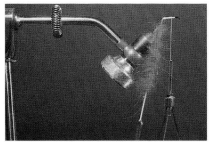

2. Twist the loop, and then wrap the thread-fur combination up the shank.

Another dubbing-loop approach involves spinning the dubbing onto the thread, doubling the thread into a loop, and spinning the loop as before. Dubbing lightly applied will really lay down; applied heavily and roughly it will provide bulk, and the dubbing will still smooth out well.

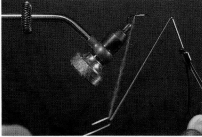

1. Spin the dubbing onto the thread as usual. With the twisting tool hooked in the thread, double the thread and secure its end with thread turns to form a loop.

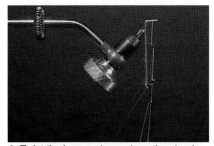

2. Twist the loop and wrap it up the shank.

Measuring

As a general rule, materials are measured against the *length* of a hook, but hackles can be measured against a hook's *gape*—the fibers should be 1 1/2 to 2 times as long as the width of the gape. But I've found that using a good hackle gauge is far more accurate and convenient than measuring hackles against a hook. Other than hackles, it is rare that anything on a dry fly is measured against a gape. Sometimes materials are measured against other materials—you will see this when you tie a fly called a Humpy—but even in this case the first

materials are usually measured against the length of a hook.

In a classic upright-wing, hackle-collar dry fly, my formula is this: The tail is equal to the full length of the hook, the wing is equal to the distance from the tip of the hook's eye to midbend, hackle starts just ahead of midshank and ends 1/16" behind the eye (unless the fly is heavily tied for rough water in which case the hackle may start at midshank or back even further), the thread head should be about 1/16" long, right behind the eye.

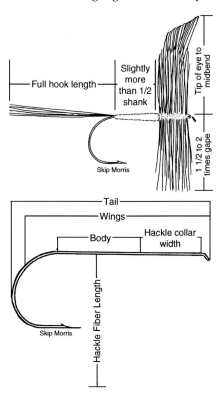

The best way I've found to mark a measured point on a material is to hold the material in such a way that the point is seen by sighting along the edge or tip of the thumb. Another method is to note the measured point and keep an eye on it until the material is positioned and secured. Some materials, such as barred hackle-tips and tail fibers, have markings that can be used to identify a measured point.

1. Note that the edge of the thumb marks the measured tie-in point.

After a material is tied in you can use the tips of your scissors, as you would a draftsman's compass, to check the length of the material against the hook—simply open the blades until the distance between the tips is equal to the distance measured, and hold the scissors firmly at their joint to secure the tip's position.

2. Using scissor tips to check measurements.

The One-Handed Whip Finish

Eventually you will probably want to learn the one-handed whip finish, because it is the fastest way to make a whip finish. Start with a half hitch. With the half-hitch loop held above the hook by your first and second fingers, turn your hand so it is palm down. Pull one side of the loop forward with your second finger. Swing the loop's side around until it and the tip of your second finger are on the near side of the hook. At this point your hand and fingers should be above the hook with the tip of your first finger on the far side of the hook and the tip of your second finger on the hook's near side. Now lower your hand, and the loop, below the hook. That's one whip-finish turn completed.

Swing the loop towards you and then above the hook again. With your palm down, repeat the previous sequence to add another whip-finish turn. When you have enough turns in place (three is about right), close the loop with a pointed object as you would for the half hitch.

1. With a half-hitch loop formed, rotate your palm down. Then draw your second finger's tip, and that side of the loop, to the near side of the hook.

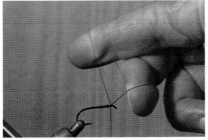

2. With your first finger guiding its side of the loop to the far side of the hook, lower your hand to complete that turn.

3. Hand lowered.

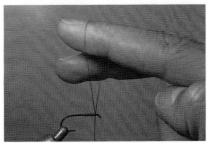

4. Swing the loop again over the hook and, with your palm down, repeat the sequence.

One-handed whip finish

1. Rotate your hand within the half hitch loop. Your palm should face down. Hook your second finger back.

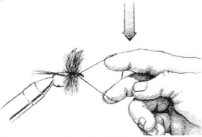

2. Lower your hand with the tip of your first finger on the far side of the hook and the tip of your second finger on the near side.

3. Swing the loop up the near side of the hook. When your hand is over the hook again, add another turn to the whip finish exactly as before.

Palmering Hackle

A "palmered" hackle is one that has been wound in open spirals; "palmering" hackle is the act of winding it in open spirals.

The simplest way to palmer a hackle is to prepare the hackle, tie it in by its stem, and wind it forward with hackle pliers. Easy.

Palmering a hackle by its tip.

This next method creates a taper of fibers from short at the rear to longer at the front. Draw the fibers back from the sides of a hackle, exposing its tip. Tie in the tip. Wind the hackle forward by its butt. The tricky part is getting the hackle started. As you first begin to wrap the hackle, reach in with your bodkin or scissor's tips and tease any wild fibers back into their natural direction, sweeping back towards the hackle's tip. Once this is under control, the hackle will usually wrap neatly. Hackle pliers can usually be omitted with this method.

1. Stroke back the fibers from a hackle's tip in preparation for palmering.

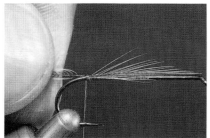

2. Tie in the hackle by its tip. Create the body that will be palmered.

3. Tease any wild hackle fibers back as you start winding the hackle.

4. Palmer the hackle by its butt.

The final method for palmering a hackle, which works well for palmering over fly bodies or abdomens (not thoraxes), is the method used on Al Troth's Elk Hair Caddis. It is demonstrated in "The Elk Hair Caddis" in section III, "Caddisfly Imitations". This method is also used on the Stimulator.

Reinforcing Peacock Herl

Fragile peacock herl is usually protected by ribbing or by a palmered hackle, but without these it can be reinforced by twisting it around the working thread. Simply tie in the herl, and then spin it and the thread in one direction between the thumbs and fingers of both hands. The twisted thread and herl will soon look almost like chenille. If the herl's quill is too wide to spin easily, bring the bobbin close, hold the herl against the bobbin's tube, and spin both.

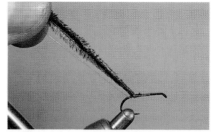

1. Tie in the herl and hold it along the thread.

2. Spin both together.

3. Hold the thread and the end of the herl as you wrap them as one up the shank.

The Reverse Pinch

The reverse pinch is merely a pinch performed with the right hand (right handers), projecting off the hook's eye, rather than with the left hand cupped over the hook's shank and bend as usual; in other words—switch hands and switch sides of the pinch loop and you've turned the pinch into the reverse pinch. The reverse pinch is sometimes used to protect fragile materials and other times because the conventional pinch just won't work.

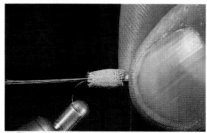

1. The reverse pinch is executed in exactly the same manner as is the standard pinch; the only change is in which hand holds the material.

2. The results of a properly executed reverse pinch.

Shaping Spun Hair

In most cases, the first cut in spun hair should be along the underside of the shank. Secure the hook by its bend in a pair of smooth-jaw pliers, old fly-tying vise jaws, midge vise jaws, or the like (you can hold the hook in your fingers, but it's awkward and a bit dangerous). Sight down the front of the hook and saw a razor blade along the shank's underside, but be careful not to cut so close that you nick the thread. Do this in more than one attempt if you fear nicking the thread—the first cut will give you a clearer view. Try to avoid touching the blade to the hook's bend, as this will quickly dull the blade.

Turn the hook upside down, decide how you want to shape the hair, and make a razor cut on each side. Do the same along the top of the hair. You now have the hair cut to its basic dimensions with a square cross section. Round the hair with razor strokes. Of course you can do all this with scissors, but I think the razor blade is easiest. Single-edged safety blades work well, but injector and double-edged blades are sharper. I like to split double-edged blades in half for safety; this can be done with tin snips.

Spun-hair heads often include a hair collar, the Jay-Dave's Hopper for example. There are two ways to trim the head while leaving the collar: Trim back to the collar and no farther, or trim a bit short of the collar and then push back the collar with your scissors' tips and trim the end of the head.

1. Make the first cut along the hook's underside.

2. Make the side cuts with the hook inverted.

3. Make the top cut.

4. Trim back the front of the body a bit, and then round out the edges.

5. Trimming a spun-hair head back to the collar.

6. Pushing back the collar to trim the rear of the head with scissors.

Spinning Deer Hair

To spin deer, elk, or caribou hair, begin with size-A rod winding thread secured to the shank. Ahead of the thread should be only bare shank. Snip a small batch of hair close to the hide (usually the bunch is about the diameter of a pencil, but this will vary with hook size). Hold the hair bunch firmly by its tips and stroke the fuzz from it with a comb. Snip the tips from the hair bunch. Hold the hair to the shank with one end down and towards the hook's eye and the other end of the hair up and slanting back; the hair should be on the near side of the hook. Take three light turns of thread around the hair and shank.

Tighten the thread *slowly* as you *slowly* release the hair bit by bit. The hair will spin around the shank and distribute itself as you tighten the thread. Once the thread is tight, draw back the hair and hold it firmly as you pull the thread tightly forward and take four turns of it against the front of the hair.

Prepare and spin on another hair bunch; then support the hair from behind as you push back on the front of the hair, compressing the second bunch back into the first. Snip, comb, spin, and compress more hair bunches until the proper amount of shank is covered. Whip finish the thread and trim its end. Remove the hook from your vise and shape the hair.

I tried everything I could think of to make hair spin, but nothing really worked until I discovered that the rate at which the hair is released is just as critical as the rate at which the thread is tightened; practice towards blending these factors for good spinning. And when you release the hair, don't just loosen your grip on it; *completely* release hairs from the side of the bunch. You should be able to see the ends of the hair springing free of your grasp.

Hair collars with spun-hair heads are best formed by combing, stacking, and then *lightly* tying in a bunch on one side of the shank, and then lightly tying in another on the other side. Hold the hair in place as you tighten the thread; lock the thread just ahead of the hair by adding four tight turns. Spin and compress any additional hair.

When adding the first batch of hair for a spun-hair body, don't spin the hair, or the tail and the hook's bend will make a mess of it; instead, trim square the butts of a hair bunch and work the bunch down around the

shank. Strive to keep the end neatly squared and set it exactly where you will want the body to end. Take two light turns of thread around the hair, hold the hair in place, and tighten—the hair's squared end will flare neatly and require little trimming, if any, later.

1. Comb a bunch of deer hair.

2. Trim the tips of the hair.

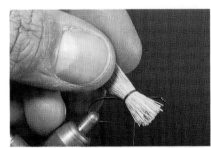

3. Hold the hair bunch to the shank and wrap the thread around it three times. (Orange thread is shown for clarity, but thread color is usually close to hair color.)

4. Gradually tighten the thread as you gradually release the hair—spinning hair.

5. A spun hair bunch.

6. Draw the hair tightly back and the thread tightly forward. Add four tight thread turns in front of the hair.

7. Compress each spun bunch into the last.

8. For a spun-hair head with a hair collar, add a combed, stacked hair bunch on one side of the hook with light thread turns, and then add a second bunch on the other side.

9. Hold the hair firmly in place as you pull the thread tight. Spin and compress any additional hair.

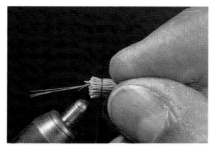

10. For the first, rearmost bunch of hair on a body, trim the bunch's butts square, take two light-tension turns of thread, work the bunch down around the shank.

11. Hold the hair firmly in place as you pull the thread tight. Draw back the butts and secure the hair as you would a spun bunch.

Split Tails

Split tails look natural and convincing. Here are three methods for creating them; try all three and then decide which you prefer.

The first method is to build a tiny ball of dubbing at the bend, strip two to four fibers from a hackle, tie in the fibers crossways to form one tail bunch, repeat the process to form the other tail bunch, trim or thread bind the fibers' butts. A couple of pointers: use very little dubbing to form the ball, as most tiers use far too much; and position the fibers to allow for torque, then they will rotate to their proper place when you tighten the thread.

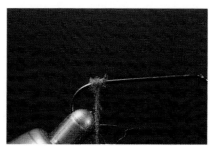

1. Create a tiny dubbing ball.

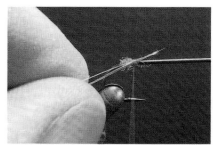

2. Tie in a bunch of fibers on the near side of the hook.

3. Tie in a bunch of fibers on the far side.

I discovered this second method in Dave Whitlock and Robert Boyle's book *The Fly-Tyer's Almanac* in the section about Rene' and Bonnie Harrop. Create a tiny ball of dubbing at the bend again, tie in four to eight hackle fibers up the shank, wrap the thread toward the bend, as the thread nears the dubbing ball divide the fibers into two groups.

1. Tie in hackle fibers (the ball of dubbing has already been formed). Divide the fibers into two groups while winding the thread to the ball.

This third method is my own. For me, it is fastest. Create a ball of *thread* at the bend; eight to ten thread turns should do it. Crisscross the thread over itself as you build it up. Run the thread up the shank and tie in a bunch of hackle fibers. Wind the thread to within three close turns of the thread ball, and then pull the fibers firmly down against the thread ball so that the fibers tip downwards; some of the fibers will stay atop the ball and others will slip to the sides. Add the last tight turns of thread against the ball; then wrap the thread forward a few turns. Release the fibers. Snip out the fibers in the center leaving a small bunch on either side.

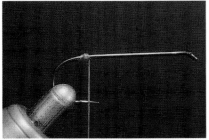

1. Build a thread ball, spiral the thread forward, and tie in the fibers.

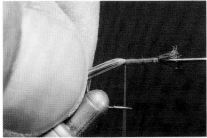

2. Wrap the thread down the fibers and shank towards the ball. As the thread nears the ball, pull the fibers tightly down and wind the thread right against the thread ball. Wrap the thread forward a few turns.

3. Snip out the center fibers leaving a small bunch on each side.

Stacking

The best way to stack hair is in a hair stacker. Here are a few pointers: Kinky hair, such as calf tail, stacks best if it is thoroughly combed, end to end. When removing hair from the stacker, grasp the hair by its tips; doing so deliberately, without a lot of extra movement, will best keep the tips squared. If your hair bunch is too large, hold it by its butts and remove fibers from the edges of the bunch.

If you are tying several flies with stacked hair, stacking hair for each one can be tedious. I prefer to stack a big bunch of hair, trim the hairs' butts square, fold a piece of

masking tape over the butts, and clamp the taped butts in a bulldog clip. Then you can snip a bunch of hairs from either side of the main bunch as needed.

1. Snip and comb a small bunch of hair, and then drop it point first into the stacker.

2. Tap the stacker.

3. Remove the hair with deliberate movements.

4. To keep the tips squared on a large batch of hair, trim the butts square and then wrap masking tape around the butts.

5. Clamp the butts in a bulldog clip.

Hair can be stacked by hand, though the results will never compare with those of a hair stacker. One way is to snip a large bunch of hair and then grasp the tips of the very longest hairs and draw those hairs from the bunch. These hairs will be somewhat squared at their tips. You can keep repeating the process as you need more hair bunches, taking the next longest hairs and then the next longest and so on.

Another method is to draw the long hairs from a small hair bunch, and then lay this bunch alongside the main bunch, tips evened. Repeat this sequence until you are satisfied with the results.

1. Draw the long fibers from a big hair bunch; these long fibers will be reasonably stacked.

2. To hand stack a single hair bunch, draw the long hairs from a small bunch.

3. Lay the new bunch alongside the old tips, squared. Repeat this sequence until you are satisfied with the results.

Tails—Hackle Fiber

The stubby, long-fibered feathers from the sides of a hackle neck, called "spade" hackles, are a fine source for hackle-fiber tails, although fibers from large neck hackles are also good. Any tail can be splayed or gathered; see "Thread Tension" in this section.

Spade hackles for tails

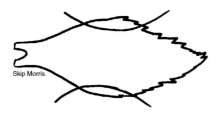

Tapered Cuts

Almost every time you cut material on a fly, you will serve yourself well to taper that cut. Blunt cuts make tiny shelves that thread slides off or refuses to climb, and blunt cuts also make bumps and gaps that knock hackles out of position and create irregular fly bodies; tapered cuts make long, low angles over which thread wraps easily and neatly, and tapered cuts provide a smooth foundation for hackles and bodies.

Where the ends of two materials meet, the best way to blend them is often to overlap their taper-cut ends; the butts of hair tails and hair wings are a good example.

Angle cut hair butts

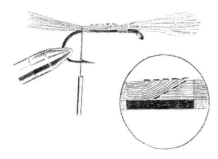

Thread Tension

As a general rule, thread turns should be as tight as possible, to create a durable fly. Dave Hughes, in his book *American Fly Tying Manual*, recommends wrapping thread onto a hook and then breaking the thread

intentionally in order to develop a sense of the thread's strength—good advice. Another way to insure tight thread wraps is to grasp a hook to support it as needed—many hooks are flexible and need support.

Exceptions to the tight-thread rule, however, are common. Setting a wing's position depends on the *right* amount of thread tension rather than maximum tension. In the case of hair wings and tails, and hackle-fiber tails, thread tension controls flare. Spongy deer-hair wings require modest thread tension to group the hair—tight thread wraps will turn deer-hair wings into shapeless fiber-riots. I prefer splayed tails on fishing flies—as opposed to "display" flies, flies tied as art for collectors—and splaying requires tight thread wraps. The point is, watch for exceptions, but when none exist, follow the tight-thread rule.

Wings—Down, Hair

Comb, stack, measure, and then tie in the hair slightly ahead of the body using the pinch (no need for the wing pinch here, since there is no flatness to preserve). Down wings usually extend at least to the edge of the bend and often quite a bit farther. Add a few tight thread turns before you proceed. If you want a well-gathered wing, now is the time to take one moderate-tension turn around the *wing only*.

Once the hair is secure, hold it firmly in place as you wrap the thread over it to the body; if these last wraps are tight, the wing will flare, but if you back off the thread tension a bit, the wing will gather. On most down-wing flies I prefer a gathered hair wing. Once the wing is secured from its tie-in point to the body, trim the hairs' butts at an angle and cover them with tight thread turns.

1. Comb, stack, and measure a bunch of hair against the hook. Secure the hair with tight turns of thread just forward of the body.

2. Take a moderate-tension thread turn around the wing only.

3. Hold the hairs in place as you wrap the thread back to the body. Trim the hairs' butts at an angle, and then bind them with tight thread turns

Wings—Down, Quill

Set two quill sections cupped together with their long sides down (some tiers prefer the long sides up, but I don't). For more information on matching quill sections, see "Wings—Upright Quill" in this section. Measure the quills so that they will extend the proper distance. Hold the cupped sections in place and tie them in using the wing pinch; add a few tight thread turns. Trim the butts of the quills at an angle and bind the trimmed butts under tight thread wraps.

For best results, tie in the wings one at a time using the wing pinch. Just make certain the first wing is firmly mounted before adding the second.

1. Once measured, tie in the wings using the wing pinch; then add several tight securing thread turns.

2. Trim the sections' butts at an angle; bind the trimmed butts under tight thread wraps.

Wings—Upright Hackle Tip

Hen-neck hackle is my all-around favorite for hackle-tip wings. With rooster-saddle, rooster-neck, and hen-neck hackles, you can simply set the tips back to back (curving away from one another), even the tips' tips, measure against the hook, and then secure the hackle tips with the pinch and a few tight thread turns.

To set the wings, grip both at their centers, draw them up and back, trim the projecting fibers at the wings' base, crease the stems of the hackle-tip wings with your thumbnail, and then add tight thread turns right up against the front of the stems to really lock the wings upright. The hackle tips can be pulled apart or pushed together as you choose. Another method is described under "The Thorax Dun"; it is a good method for upright hen-saddle wings and some others.

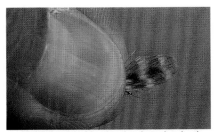

1. Hold the hackle tips back to back, tips even, measure the tips against the hook, tie in the tips using the pinch; then add several tight thread turns to really secure the tips.

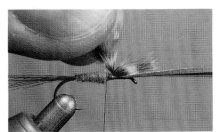

2. Create a tail and body. Pull back the tips and trim the fibers at their base.

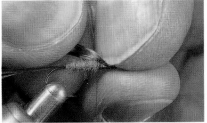

3. Crease the hackle tips' stems with your thumbnail.

4. Add tight turns of thread against the front of the tips' base to secure their position. Adjust the width of the wings. Here is how hackle-tip wings should look.

Wings—Upright Hair

Comb, stack, measure, and tie in a bunch of hair using the pinch (no need to use the wing pinch here since there is no flatness to preserve). With slippery hard hairs like calf tail and buck tail, 3/0 thread will help you achieve plenty of thread tension. Set the wings upright and divide them as described under "Wings—Wood Duck" in this section.

1. Tie in the hair bunch using the pinch, crease the hair upright with your thumbnail, split the hair; crisscross it with thread, and then set the hair wings upright as you would with wood duck.

2. Grouping hair wings is accomplished by adding moderate-tension thread turns at each wing's base.

The Wing Pinch

The wing pinch is a variation of the regular pinch. As the pinch loop is tightened, the pinch finger and thumb are slid down slightly to help compress the wing neatly; care is taken to preserve the wings' flatness. It also helps to draw the thread not only down but also slightly towards you.

1. As you tighten the loop, slide your finger and thumb slightly down around the shank.

Wing pinch

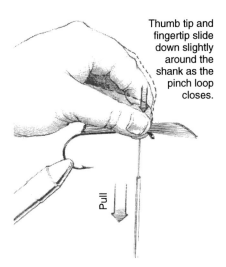

Thumb tip and fingertip slide down slightly around the shank as the pinch loop closes.

Pull

Wings—Upright Quill

Begin with two matched quills; "matched," regarding quills, means one from a left wing and one from a right and both similar in size and form. The most common dry-fly quills are duck and mottled turkey.

Snip a section from the same part of each quill; the sections should be equal in width. Hold the sections together, curving apart, tips even. Hold the quills to the tie-in point with their long sides down. Tie in the quills using the wing pinch. Add a few tight thread turns. Lift the quills up and back and crease them at their base with your thumbnail. Add tight thread turns up against the wings' base to secure the wings upright.

That's it. You can adjust the width of the wings' split with a tug or two. Some tiers set quill wings in the same manner I've described for wood-duck wings.

1. A matched pair of duck quills and the wing sections cut from them.

2. The quill sections properly held for mounting.

3. Measure the quill sections against the hook.

4. Tie in the quill sections with the wing pinch.

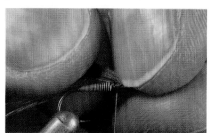

5. Create the tail and body; then crease the quill sections' base with your thumbnail.

6. Add tight thread wraps to set the quill sections' position.

7. Properly set, upright quill-wings.

Wings—Wood Duck

Wood-duck feathers are a soft lemon yellow with delicate barring; they are quite lovely. Wood duck wings are traditional, and worth mastering.

To start, strip the fuzz from the base of a single wood-duck feather, and then strip one 3/16" section from each side of the stem. If the tips of the sections are not squared on the feather, you can square them by drawing the sections to a different angle to the stem before stripping them. Proceed from here as shown in the photographs and illustrations.

1. Wood-duck feathers: one stripped, and one with a set of wing sections removed.

2. Take up the sections, back to back, tips evened. Measure the sections against the hook, and then tie in the sections using the wing pinch. Snip the butts at an angle and bind them with thread.

3. Add the tail and body. Lift the wings and build thread against their front to support them. Sight down the front of the wings and divide them, and then add crisscrossing thread turns as shown in the illustrations.

4. Set the wings up one at a time with thread, as shown in the illustrations. Here is a properly set pair of wood-duck wings.

Wood Duck Wings

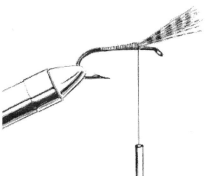

1. Tie in the wood-duck Sections using the Pinch.

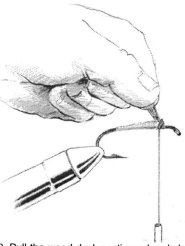

2. Pull the wood-duck sections sharply back and build thread turns at their base.

3.Sight down the front of the wood-duck fibers and divide them into two groups with the tips of your scissors. Pull the groups firmly to the sides

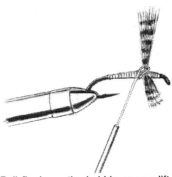

7. Pull firmly on the bobbin as you lift the wing flatly into position. Once the wing is set, maintain tension on the thread as you add three tight thread turns. **Remember**: Thread direction has been reversed.

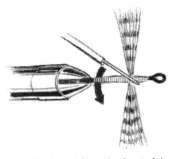

4. Pass the thread from the front of the near wing to the rear of the far wing.

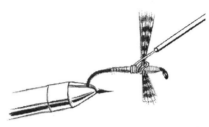

8. Pass the thread between the wings again and then around the near wing. Raise and set the near wing as you did the far one. Now the thread is back to its original direction.

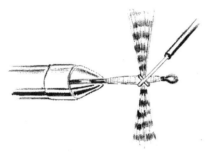

5. Pass the thread beneath the hook and then from the rear of the near wing to the front of the far wing.

9. The wings are set.

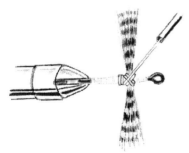

6. Pass the thread beneath the hook and then from the front of the near wing to the rear of the far wing again. Add two thread turns just behind the wings. Pass the thread from the rear of the near wing to the front of the far wing again; **then, pass the thread around the outside of the far wing and then over the top of the hook and down the near side**. Thread direction is now reversed.

XI

HACKLE—
STILL THE STANDARD

When I began fly fishing in the early '60s, virtually all dry flies had hackle collars. Since then the evolution of the dry fly has been vigorous. We have seen No Hackles, Comparaduns, bullet heads, wing-and-body-only caddises—all hackleless dry flies and all in common use. Yet for all this, most dry flies set atop our trout streams and lakes today still bear hackles.

Types Of Hackles

The dry-fly tier must understand hackles. A good place to start is hackle types. Virtually all hackles for dry flies come from chicken roosters. Hen hackles and hackles from birds other than chickens are occasionally used in dry flies, but only as wings and such; rarely is any feather other than a rooster hackle wrapped on a dry fly to suggest legs.

There are two parts of the rooster that produce dry-fly hackles: the rump, or saddle; and the neck, or cape. Saddle hackles can be excellent. They tend to be fine-stemmed and long—both are desirable characteristics in a dry-fly hackle. The drawback of saddle hackle is that a single saddle patch usually contains only two or, at most, three hackle sizes; this means that several saddle patches are required if the tier is to tie the full range of dry-fly sizes. And some hackle sizes are tough to come by in saddles.

Excellent hackles can also be found on necks, along with a broad, complete range of hackle sizes. Most tiers choose necks, and some of these tiers supplement necks with saddles.

Left to right: hen saddle hackle, hen neck hackle, rooster neck hackle, rooster saddle hackle (on the far right and across the bottom).

Hackle Quality

Once you've made the decision as to which type of hackle you want—saddle or neck—your next concern will be hackle quality. Cheap hackles are usually imported, and I hesitate to recommend them for any dry fly. The best dry-fly hackles are from roosters bred and grown specifically for their feathers. The finest hackles are, understandably, expensive.

Hackles are graded as to quality: #1 is best, #2 is moderate quality, and #3 is the lowest quality. I find that #2 hackles are usually the best balance of quality and price. But #1 hackles, especially the best, are impressive, and tying with them is a joy.

Paying an appropriate price for a tying-bred neck or saddle patch from a reputable breeder, and sold by a reputable seller, is good insurance; but the best insurance that you will get good hackle lies in your ability to recognize it. Here is what to look for: The fibers of good hackles are stiff and dense; poor hackles often have fibers that are soft or sparse or both. Good hackles have long stretches of fibers similar in length; poor hackles may have only a short stretch of such fibers, or no such stretch, only a tip-to-butt taper. Good hackles have fine, strong, flexible, consistent stems; poor hackles may have stems that are thick, brittle, and inclined to twist under the motions of tying. Some hackles have stems that are spiraled; this you can see in the spiraling of the fibers.

Hoffman and Metz are the best-known names in quality hackle, but other breeders are gaining distinction.

Hackle Colors
And Markings

Hackle necks of various colors and markings tend to have different characteristics; the exception to this is dyed hackles, which probably all start out white or barred. In my experience, these characteristics are associated with different hackles: Barred hackles have fine stems and dense fibers, brown and ginger hackles have thick stems, and blue dun hackles have fine fibers.

I'll probably discover other tendencies in years to come, and breeding will surely alter the current picture, but right now that's how I see it. Saddles are saddles, and I haven't noticed any significant differences from one color or marking to the next.

Keep an eye out for unusual hackle colors and markings; I have a barred ginger neck that I save only for display flies, and I saw a cree neck recently that is on my wish list. There is really no reason to be strict about patterns and hackles—though a pattern calls for ginger hackle, a barred ginger will probably be just as effective—perhaps more.

Here is a description of standard hackle colors and markings:

Badger: cream to tan with a black, tapered stripe running up the center along the stem.
Black: black.
Blue dun: a bluish gray, from pale to dark.
Brown: brown, sometimes reddish.

Grizzly Ginger

Badger

Brown

Black

Ginger

Grizzly

Furnace

White

Blue Dun

Cream

Hackle Colors and Markings

Brian Rose Photo

Cream: cream.

Furnace: the same as badger but darker, some kind of brown with a black stripe.

Ginger: light ginger is pale, even almost cream; dark ginger is a golden tan.

Grizzly: alternating white and black stripes across the feather.

White: white.

Preparing Hackle

Recognizing, selecting, and obtaining good hackle is half of the preparation for tying good flies with it; the other half is the way in which you prepare the hackle itself. All hackles have soft, webby fibers at their base, and these webby fibers should be stripped to the bare stem. On even the best neck hackles, at least the full lower third of the stem should be stripped; on most neck hackles this becomes about half. Saddles are another matter, but you get the idea.

The neatest, quickest method I've found for stripping a hackle's base is to grasp the feather firmly at the beginning of the area to be stripped, draw the hackle by its tip through your grasp in turn stroking the fibers out, and then strip the fibers from one side and then the other. The other problem with hackle bases is that their fibers tend to be longer than those in the useful "sweet spot," the tier's name for the stretch of even-length fibers.

1. Stroke out from the stem the fibers to be stripped

2. Hold the hackle by its stem and strip one side of the stem's base, then the other.

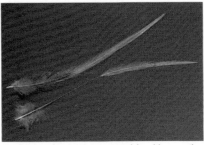

3. On top is an unprepared hackle; on the bottom, one properly prepared.

Finding The Sweet Spot

Finding the sweet spot is easy. The same tool that helps you size hackle will help you find its sweet spot: the hackle gauge. Slide a good hackle across the post of a hackle gauge. Start at the hackle's butt. First, some downy, useless fibers will cross the post. Then some stiffer fibers, still with web, will follow; these stiffer fibers will steadily and rapidly diminish in length. Next will be a stretch of fibers equal, or nearly so, in length—this is the sweet spot. At the end of the sweet spot the fibers will quickly diminish in length to the hackle's point.

That's a typical hackle's shape: wide, webby, and quickly tapered at the base, constant for a while, and then tapered to a point. You can see this by stroking the fibers away from the stem, but a hackle gauge will tell you this best.

1. It's easy to find the sweet spot on this hackle with its fibers stroked out from its stem.

The Basic Dry Fly Hackle Collar—Traditional Method

The traditional method for creating a basic hackle collar is simple, and it makes a perfectly good fly that will catch fish. Stick with it if you like. The method I use has come to me over years of production tying and display-fly tying. With it I have created my neatest, most-elegant hackle collars. Regarding fish-catching qualities of the two methods, I doubt there is any difference. Here is the traditional method for creating a basic hackle collar:

1. Tie in two prepared hackles by their stems at the rear of the hackle area. Trim the stems and bind them with thread. Advance the thread to about 1/16" behind the hook's eye.

2. Clamp your hackle pliers onto the tip of one hackle and wind that hackle in tight, close turns to the thread's end. Secure the hackle's tip with three tight turns of thread. Remove the hackle pliers from the hackle's tip.

3. Wind the second hackle through the first. As you wind the second hackle, zig zag it back and forth to allow trapped fibers to escape.

4. Secure the tip of the second hackle as you did the tip of the first. Trim both tips closely, and then build a thread head (see "The Thread Head" in section X, "Basic Techniques").

The Basic Dry Fly Hackle Collar—My Method

Here is my method for creating a basic hackle collar:

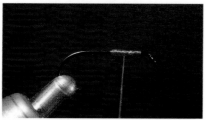

1. Wrap a layer of thread from 1/16" behind the eye to *just short* of midshank, and then wrap the thread forward to *just short* of the center of the first thread layer. These thread wraps help you guage the wing and hackle locations. Tie in the wing here. (The first thread layer should be longer if you desire a wider hackle collar, shorter if you desire a slimmer one.)

2. With the body, tail, and wing complete, secure the first hackle atop the hook with several tight turns of thread. The hackle should be on its edge, butt angling forward on the near side of the hook, tip end angling back on the far side, cupped face (the concave side) to the rear.

3. Secure the second hackle beneath the hook with several tight turns of thread. The hackle should be on its edge, butt angling forward on the *far* side of the hook, tip end angling back on the *near* side, cupped face again to the rear.

4. Work the thread forward, toward the hook's eye, binding the hackles' stems. Guide the stem from the *top* hackle down the near side of the hook; guide the *bottom* hackle's stem underneath and in line with the shank. Trim the top hackle's stem when it reaches down alongside and below the near wing; trim the end of the stem at an angle for a tapered cut. Continue wrapping the thread forward over the bottom hackle's stem. Just ahead of the wings, trim the bottom hackle's stem at an angle. Continue wrapping the thread to about 1/16" behind the eye.

TYING IN, TRIMMING, AND BINDING HACKLE STEMS

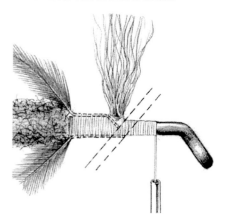

5. Clamp the jaws of your hackle pliers well down onto the *top* hackle's tip. Begin wrapping the top hackle forward leaving a thin space between turns. Leave a thin space between the hackle and the rear of the wings; then increase the angle of the hackle's stem as you bring it down the far side of the wings, beneath the hook, and then right up against the front of the wings. Continue wrapping the hackle forward; now you can decrease the spaces between turns.

Secure the hackle's tip atop the hook's shank with three tight thread turns, just behind the eye. Closely trim the stem and any projecting fibers (or you can trim this tip when you trim the second hackle's tip).

6. Take up the bottom hackle in your hackle pliers and wrap it one-half turn to the top of the hook. Bring the bottom hackle forward to lock in its stem ahead of the top hackle's stem; now the bottom hackle is in front of the top hackle, and lies in the slot between the turns of stem.

7. Wrap the bottom hackle forward at the same angle you used to wrap the top hackle. If the angles are close, the bottom hackle will find its way into the slot between turns of the top hackle's stem. Remember that you left a slot immediately behind the wings, but wrapped the first hackle right up against the front of the wings. When the bottom hackle's tip is just behind the eye, secure and trim it as you did the top hackle's tip. Build a thread head (see "The Thread Head" in section I, "Essential Techniques").

WRAPPING DRY FLY HACKLES

1. Take up a hackle in your hackle pliers and wrap it forward in slightly open spirals.

2. Secure the first hackle's tip with thread turns . Wrap the second hackle's stem in the spaces between the turns of the first hackle's stem.

A few pointers. Keep the hackle pliers in line with the hackle's stem as you wrap it; an angle weakens the stem. Develop a sense of how much tension a hackle stem will stand and work near this limit to insure a tight, durable hackle collar. The bottom hackle's stem can be guided into the slot between turns of the top hackle both by sight and by feel. Hackle turns should be close to the base of the wings, even against it, but watch that those turns don't knock the wings out of position. If you want a neat hackle, expect to unwind and then rewind one once in a while. A standard hackle collar will take a total of four to six turns behind the wings and eight to ten turns in front of them (half this many turns of each hackle, of course); rough-water flies may require saddle hackles, or three neck hackles, in up to twenty-one turns.

A typical hackle collar should start just ahead of midshank; a rough-water collar may start *at* midshank or even behind it; short collars for slow-water flies may start around two-thirds up the shank.

Parachute Hackles

Because there doesn't seem to be a traditional method for creating parachute hackles, I offer mine only. My method is different from any I've seen. Some tiers avoid parachute hackles, finding them awkward and frustrating to execute, but my method is so easy to execute that I often tie a parachute fly in my hands, without a vise, at clinics and demonstrations.

The complaints are that the wing flops around, that holding the wing at its top for support makes hackle wrapping slow, that tying off the hackle's tip is awkward, and that the hackle slips free under the stresses of casting and fishing.

I'll show you how to wrap a neat parachute hackle without ever having to support the wing, how to tie off the hackle's tip and create a thread head easily, and how to make a parachute hackle that is just as durable as a conventional hackle collar.

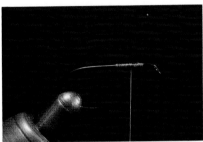

1. Start the thread 1/16" behind the hook's eye and wrap it back to just short of midshank creating a layer of thread. Wrap the thread forward to *just past* the center of the first thread layer. Here is where you will tie in the wing.

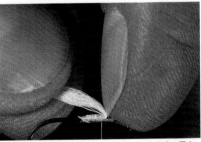

2. Measure the wing and then tie it in. Trim the wing's butts at an angle and bind them with thread. Set the wing upright by pulling it sharply back and creasing its base with your thumbnail.

3. Take two turns of thread around the base of the wing only (not around the hook's shank). Pull the thread turns tight (you can hold the wing if needed). Wrap the thread *lightly* up the base of the wing in close turns; this will gather the wing and provide a hackle base. Wrap up the wing at *least* a full 1/16" (most tiers forget that it takes just as much space to wrap a hackle vertically as horizontally). Wrap the thread lightly down the wing's base in close turns.

4. Keep the thread tight as you pull it back to secure the wing upright. The thread should go back and down the far side of the hook. Keep the thread tight as you take a few tight turns of the thread to lock it and the wing in place. Repeat the thread setting of the wing if necessary until the wing is at a right angle to the shank. For insurance that the wing won't later roll to one side, you can first set the wing with the thread on the near side of the hook, and then set the wing with the thread on the far side; this way, the wing is pulled from both sides.

7. Take up the hackle's tip in your hackle pliers. Wrap the hackle down the wing's base in close, consecutive counterclockwise turns (right-handers). When you reach the fly's body, drape the hackle's tip across the shank just behind the eye and let your hackle pliers hang on the hook's far side. It helps to get your eyes down level with the plane of the hackle as you wrap it. Also, be certain that the hackle is wrapped in the right direction; then the thread's torque will, rather than loosen them, tighten the hackle wraps slightly.

5. Hold a prepared (sized and stripped) hackle vertically along the wing's base; the hackle's stripped stem should end at the top of the wing's thread-wrapped base. Hold the hackle by its stem just beneath the shank. Wrap the thread up the stem and the wing's base; because of the added stiffness of both the first thread wraps and the hackle's stem, you can now apply heavy tension to the thread—without having to support the wing. Wrap the thread back down the wing's base.

8. Reach your left thumb, first finger, and second finger (right-handers) beneath the hackle fibers that project over the hook's eye. As you draw these fibers up and back from the eye, take three tight thread turns around the shank, catching the hackle's tip in the process—now the hackle's tip is secured.

6. Draw the hackle's butt end back, secure it to the hook's shank with thread turns, and trim the stem. Add the tails, and create a body from the tails to just in front of the wing (leave bare shank behind the eye for a neat thread head).

9. Closely trim the hackle's tip. Continue to add thread, building a tapered thread head. Release the hackle fibers; they will now stay back from the eye on their own. Complete the thread head as usual. When the thread head is complete and head cement is hard, tug hackles and wing back into position.

XII

DRY-FLY MATERIALS

It is likely that every material ever used in fly tying has been used in some dry-fly pattern. What makes a material specific to dry flies if any material can be used in a dry fly? I think the common denominator is buoyancy—desirable in a dry fly, undesirable in a nymph. There are exceptions, and the most significant of these are flies that imitate partially hatched insects. Such flies are often designed so that part of the fly sinks and part of it floats—the sinking portion is treated more as an artificial nymph than as a dry fly. Other exceptions to the buoyancy rule include materials that offer special benefits—the Clark's Stonefly has a gold mylar body which, though it adds no buoyancy, provides flash. But exceptions are easily recognized; the vast majority of dry flies are meant to float high and long, and this is accomplished through the use of buoyant materials.

No list of dry-fly materials can ever be complete—there are too many that are seldom-used, outdated, or little-known. So here is a current collection of the popular materials you will see in today's dry flies.

Cements

For cementing the thread head of any fly—dry fly, nymph, streamer—there are many good commercial head cements. (The term "head cement" refers to any glue or cement used on a thread head or thread collar.) My favorite is Crystal Clear Epoxy glue made by Epoxy Coatings and marketed as a rod-builder's glue (see "The Thread Head" in section I, "Essential Techniques"). Dave's Flexament and Tuffilm (Tuffilm is available in art stores) have proved valuable for toughening fly wings and for other uses.

Threads

For all-around tying of trout flies there is 8/0 and 6/0 thread—I especially like 8/0; for big flies, or flies that require lots of thread tension, there is 3/0; and for flaring and spinning deer hair I prefer size-A rod-winding thread. There are special tiny-fly threads, but I use 8/0 for even the smallest hooks.

Fly-tying threads are available prewaxed or unwaxed. Prewaxed threads are lightly waxed and most tiers choose them; Fly-tying wax can be purchased separately and added as needed to either prewaxed or unwaxed threads. A full color range of threads is fun to work with, but I feel that brown and tan are all you really need.

Feathers

The predominant dry-fly feather is the hackle—the vast majority of dry flies have it in their makeup. The hackle I speak of is from a rooster's neck or rump and is wound around a hook's shank or a wing's base; this radiates the hackle's fibers to suggest insect legs. For a study of the dry-fly rooster hackle and its use, see section XI, "Hackle—Still The Standard."

For hackle-tip and shaped-hackle wings, the best source I've found is hen neck, whose hackles are broad and hold their shape. Other feathers that can be matched or clumped for dry-fly wings include body feathers such as turkey flats, wood duck, teal, and mallard. Duck and turkey primary wing feathers make handsome upright wings, or they can be paired and layed back, or a single section can simply be rolled around the body to suggest the low wings of grasshoppers and caddisflies. Primary feathers are often called "quills."

In a flurry of excitement American fly tiers have recently discovered the cul de canard feather which comes from the buttocks of a duck (or whatever a duck has in place of buttocks). Cul de canard is extremely buoyant, but the durability of that buoyancy and the value of this feather to fly tiers and fly fishers awaits the verdict that only time can deliver.

Furs

Furs and synthetic dubbings are used to create fly bodies. Furs such as badger, muskrat, mole, otter, and versatile dyed and natural rabbit offer only fair buoyancy, and that only with the aid of fly floatant. Their value in a dry fly is their fine texture. Antron and polypropylene dubbings are becoming very popular for dry-fly bodies; these synthetics offer durability, buoyancy, and a wide selection of colors. Blends of natural fur and synthetic dubbing are gaining fly tiers' favor.

Yarns

Yarn is mainly a nymph material, but buoyant synthetic yarns are changing that, polypropylene and antron yarns in particular. It's hard to beat yarns for creating a tough, thick fly body with ease, especially on big flies where dubbing can be slow. Even woven polypropylene macrame yarns are catching on for extended fly bodies.

Materials

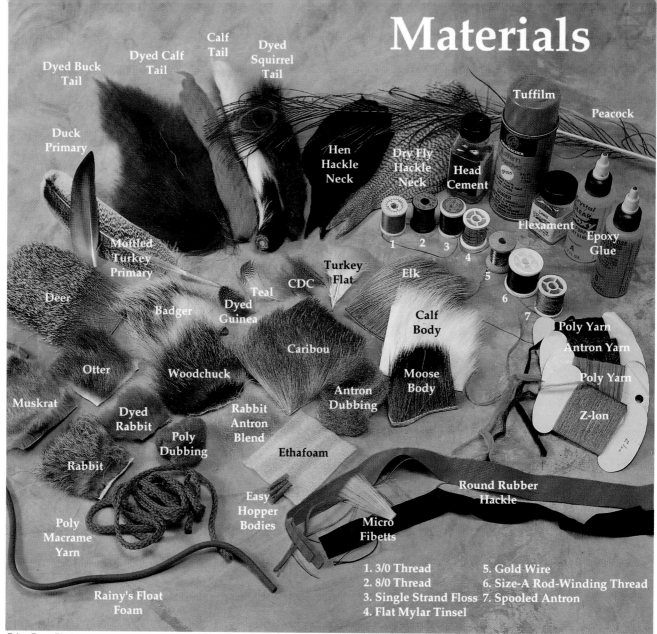

Dyed Buck Tail · Dyed Calf Tail · Calf Tail · Dyed Squirrel Tail · Tuffilm · Peacock · Duck Primary · Hen Hackle Neck · Dry Fly Hackle Neck · Head Cement · Flexament · Epoxy Glue · Mottled Turkey Primary · Turkey Flat · Elk · CDC · Deer · Teal · Dyed Guinea · Badger · Calf Body · Moose Body · Poly Yarn · Antron Yarn · Poly Yarn · Otter · Woodchuck · Caribou · Antron Dubbing · Z-lon · Muskrat · Dyed Rabbit · Rabbit Antron Blend · Poly Dubbing · Ethafoam · Round Rubber Hackle · Rabbit · Easy Hopper Bodies · Micro Fibetts · Poly Macrame Yarn · Rainy's Float Foam

1. 3/0 Thread
2. 8/0 Thread
3. Single Strand Floss
4. Flat Mylar Tinsel
5. Gold Wire
6. Size-A Rod-Winding Thread
7. Spooled Antron

Brian Rose Photo

Another dry-fly use for synthetic yarns is to create wings and to suggest the shucks of partially hatched insects. Unwoven spooled antron, "poly" (polypropylene) yarn, sparkle poly yarn, and Z-lon make fine wings and shucks. Bright yarns can also increase the visibility of almost any dry fly (see section IX, "Highly Visible Flies").

Hairs

Practically all fly-tying hair is buoyant enough to make good dry-fly tails and wings. Hair with tiny air pockets–deer, elk, and cariboo–is especially buoyant and can be flared and then trimmed to shape for bodies and heads.

For wings and tails, I like calf-tail hair for its softness, durability, and the spread of its kinky tips; some tiers prefer calf-body hair which is straighter than calf tail and is especially good for the wings of tiny flies. Other popular and proven wing-and-tail hairs include deer, elk, buck tail, squirrel tail, moose body, and badger and mink guard hairs.

Of the hairs used for flaring and shaping, deer is the traditional choice, elk is too course for small flies but tough and buoyant in big ones, and caribou is a bit fragile but flares best.

Various Materials

Light weight makes mylar tinsel practical in a dry fly; metal tinsels, previously the only kind, are heavy. Because of its use in the popular Elk Hair Caddis, fine wire is now used sometimes to secure and reinforce hackle.

Where dubbing's fluffiness tends to add too much thickness, floss makes a slim, quick-to-form fly body. Peacock herl has qualities easier to see than to describe; no other material has them, thus peacock remains a valuable dry-fly component. Foam of all kinds— flat, round, thick, thin, pliant, stiff, fine-celled, coarse-celled, blank, colored—is useful for all types of floating flies. Some foams are available from fly shops; others must be searched out. Synthetic tails, similar to hackle fibers but tougher, are now in common use. Rubber strands, often called "rubber hackle" or "rubber legs," are catching on for imitating insect legs, especially the finer, rounded strands.

XIII

DRY-FLY TOOLS

The notion of a complete set of tools for tying nymphs, another set for dry flies, and so on is silly—nearly all the tools listed here are used for tying all types of flies, including dry flies. But some tools—the hackle gauge and hackle pliers come immediately to mind—are used mainly for tying dry flies; others are used in ways particular to tying dry flies. So the following list addresses fly-tying tools from the dry-fly perspective.

The Vise

If a fly-tying vise is sturdy, holds a wide range of hooks firmly, opens and tightens easily, and allows plenty of tying access, it is a good vise.

Vises are clamp-mounted or base-mounted. Clamps are more secure, but I like my base-mounted vise because it is portable, and secure enough.

"Rotary" vises allow you to rotate the jaws to inspect a fly and work on it from all sides; "stationary" vises have a set jaw position. I tied with a good stationary vise for many years and it served me honorably—I even tied flies on it that won competitions—but now I'm sold on my rotary vise. I guess that says it: A stationary vise is fine (and usually reasonably priced), but a rotary vise has some advantages that grow on you.

Scissors

Don't skimp—good scissors are essential. And get scissors made especially for fly tying. I like scissors with finely serrated edges which hold onto materials.

Bobbins

A bobbins holds thread, floss, and sometimes other materials. It's crazy to consider tying without a thread bobbin. One is enough, but more is handy. I increasingly use a floss bobbin. A thread bobbin will handle floss, but the floss bobbin's wide tube with a flared end is best.

Hackle Pliers

My rule regarding hackle pliers is this: Get some and use them. As to the many hackle-plier styles, if a pair holds the hackle securely and has a loop for the tier's finger, it's a good pair. Some tiers don't use the finger loop in hackle pliers, so they don't miss it if it's absent. I still prefer the classic rounded-jaw, all-metal pliers.

Hackle Guage

Sizing hackles against a hook is slow and cumbersome compared with sizing hackles on a hackle gauge. Get a hackle gauge.

Hair Stacker

A wide stacker will stack a little hair or a lot; a slim stacker will stack only a small bunch of hair, so I prefer a wide stacker. Besides, it is the separation of the hairs that makes stacking efficient, and a wide stacker allows the hairs to really separate. For my own tying, a hair stacker is a requirement.

Light

Some kind of adjustable light that will pour lots of light down on the jaws of your vise is a must. Plenty of ambient light also helps.

Optional Tools

We just covered the tools you need; I'd be reluctant to tie without them. The next tools are optional but useful.

Magnifier

Mother Nature banks heavily in some of us, lightly in others, but over the years she slowly empties all her accounts. So if your eyesight is impaired, either by design or by Nature's withdrawals, your tying will benefit from some sort of magnifier. Even keen eyesight may demand magnification for the tying of tiny flies.

There are different types of magnifiers. Arm-mounted lenses, some with built-in light, work well. Another option is reading glasses, which are essentially magnifiers. Glasses with magnification of 2.5 may be enough for slightly limited sight and standard-size trout flies; for the same sight and tiny flies, magnification of 3.5 to 4.5 may be required. Right now, my favorite is a binocular magnifier, the headband, hinged hood type that jewelers use. They even fit over glasses.

A binocular magnifier.

Pliers

Small-jawed, flat-nose pliers make barb smashing easy. Any pliers of this description will work; fly shops often carry them.

Bodkin

The bodkin is a needle mounted into a post. They are handy, but a hatpin will substitute.

Carol Morris Photo

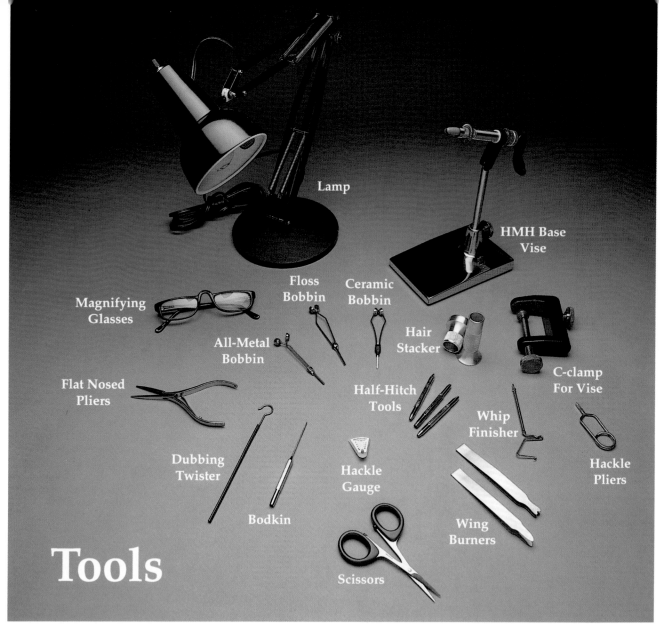

Tools

Brian Rose Photo

The image shows various fly-tying tools labeled: Lamp, HMH Base Vise, Floss Bobbin, Ceramic Bobbin, Magnifying Glasses, Hair Stacker, All-Metal Bobbin, C-clamp For Vise, Flat Nosed Pliers, Half-Hitch Tools, Whip Finisher, Hackle Pliers, Dubbing Twister, Hackle Gauge, Bodkin, Wing Burners, Scissors.

Blender

Useful for blending various types and colors of dubbing. A household liquid blender will work—dig out the wet fur, press it between paper towels, and let it air dry—but the easiest is a dry blender; fly shops carry them.

Dubbing Twister

This is used for twisting dubbing in a thread loop. I rarely use one for tying dry flies and only slightly more often when tying other flies. But a dubbing twister is sometimes extremely useful. A half-straightened paper clip is a fair substitute.

Old Scissors

You can cut hard materials—wire, nylon leader for extended bodies—with the insides of your scissors (never use the tips to cut hard materials), but with worn or old scissors there is no danger of damaging the tips—they're already shot.

Material Holder

Usually a spring or a clip. They hold long materials out of the tier's way. I'm sold on material holders. As my friend Gordon Nash points out, the spring holder allows you to remove materials from it in any order, which the clip does not.

Whip Finisher

A tool that helps the tier execute a whip finish. I prefer using my fingers, but I know tiers who like and use whip finishers.

Half-Hitch Tool

As with the whip finisher, I use my fingers for this work. But some of my friends like and use half-hitch tools.

Wing Burner

Allows you to burn feathers to wing shapes. They are handy and fun to play with, but not required.

Bobbin Threader

I no longer use one. If I can't suck a thread end out a bobbin's tube I'll insert a loop of nylon leader. Besides, there are rumors that a metal-loop threader can scratch a bobbin's tube, and *that* can fray thread.

Hair Packer

Helps tiers compress spun hair. Be certain that yours has a small hole—a large-hole packer compresses poorly. I still don't use a hair packer, but many good tiers do.

DRY-FLY HOOKS

In my first fly-tying book, *Fly Tying Made Clear and Simple*, I explained how fly hooks are sized, classified—the works. Rather than reword something I've already said to the best of my ability, here is my best explanation of fly hooks:

Hooks Simplified

To understand hooks, it is best to start with a bit of anatomy. The "eye" is the loop of wire at one end of a hook; the "shank" is a hook's long, straight middle section; the "bend" is the widely curved wire at the opposite end from the eye; the "point" is the sharp, penetrating point at the end of the bend; the "gap," also called a "gape," is the distance between the hook's point and shank; and the "barb" is the tiny upturned shard, just behind the point, that is meant to keep a hook from slipping out of a fish (a suspect theory we will soon discuss further).

There are only three basic considerations for selecting a hook: size, length, and wire. Other considerations are minor, and usually subjective, though we will explore them as well. But first let's take a look at the basic three.

Hooks are sized by numbers. The numbers are almost always even (though a very few hooks are sized with odd numbers, for reasons I fail to understand). The tiniest hooks have the largest numbers—a size 14 hook is about average for trout flies, a size 20 is tiny, and a size 26 is so small that most anglers will never tie or fish with one. Big trout hooks start at size 8, but past size 1, the sizing starts at 1/0 and from that point on, hooks get **larger** as their numbers get larger—I'm sorry, but they do. From 1/0 on up, the " /0" follows each number. You won't have to worry about anything with an "/0" behind it in this book.

Hook length is signified with a number, followed by an"X," followed by a "long" or "short." The explanation is that there is a standard length for each hook size and that the numbers,"X"s, and "long"s and "short"s tell you how far, and in which direc-

tion, a hook deviates from that standard. If your hook is "standard length" or "regular length," that's obvious. However, if your hook is 1X long, that means that your hook is one size longer than regular length—but what does *that* mean? In theory, it means that this hook is the same length as a hook one size larger; but in fact, it means whatever that particular manufacturer says it means. What is significant is that a hook 1X long is slightly longer than normal, a hook 2X long is slightly longer yet, and a hook 8X long is really long. All this works in reverse for the "short" designations—"1X short" is slightly short and"2X short" is slightly shorter and so on. Hook length does not affect the hook's bend or gape; they remain constant, and the hook's eye isn't a consideration in determining length.

Hook wire is usually chosen to help a fly sink or float—thick wire is heavy and makes a fly sink; thin wire is lighter and helps a fly float. Occasionally thick wire is chosen simply for strength; this usually means big, powerful fish—bass, tarpon, and the like. Thin wire is called "fine" and thick wire is called "heavy." The fineness or heaviness of wire is determined, once again, with "X"s, and once again, all this begins with the assumption that there is a model, an acknowledged norm—in this case, a standard hook wire for each hook size. And "standard" is the word for it—a hook with wire between fine and heavy has "standard wire." "1X heavy" means a hook with wire meant for a hook one size larger, "2X heavy" for a hook two sizes larger, "1X light" for a hook one size smaller and so on. This business too, I suspect, varies from one manufacturer to the next.

So how do you decide exactly the size, length, and wire thickness of your hook? Easy: follow the pattern. A

"pattern" is simply a list-description of materials for a given fly; more on this later.

Time for a review. If your fly's pattern calls for a hook that is size 12, 2X long, 1X heavy, what does this mean? Stop and try to answer this before you read on. Here is what it means: The hook you want is of about average size for trout, it is two increments longer than the standard, and it is formed of wire that would normally be used on a hook one size larger. How did you do?

There are some secondary hook considerations, but although there are accepted guidelines to cover them, most experienced fly tiers decide for themselves. The hooks designated for the flies in this book generally conform to these guidelines. The first of these secondary considerations is the angle of the eye. If the eye tips up, it is an "up eye" or "turned-up eye"; if the eye is straight, in line with the shank, it is a "ring eye"; if the eye tips down, it is a "down eye" or "turned-down eye." Everyone used to use turned-down-eye hooks for almost everything except Atlantic salmon and steelhead, but a lot of anglers now use the other eye styles for all kinds of fishing—personal preference. There are also variations in eye construction, but I've found them usually to be of only minor significance, and if a special eye style is important for a certain type of fishing—the tapered loop-eye of Atlantic-salmon and steelhead hooks is a good example—you'll hear about it plenty.

Another secondary consideration is the shape of the bend. There are "Limerick," "Perfect," "Sneck," and "Sproat" bends and these sometimes go by different names. There are probably other bends of which I am unaware. The pattern may advise, but anglers usually make this a personal decision. As Dave Hughes wrote in his *American Fly Tying Manual*, "Hook bends are mostly a matter of eye appeal, though there are endless debates about the hooking qualities of each kind....The Viking, Sproat, and Limerick are the three most popular styles; they've all been around for years, and they all hook and hold fish well."

Watch for abbreviations. "1X short" may become "1XS," "2X light" may be "2XL," "turned up eye" may be "TUE" and so on. But it's all pretty logical.

There is also the matter of manufacturers who disregard the rules. You look through their catalogs for a 6X long hook and the only thing close says "streamer-bucktail hook"; that's alright though, because you are tying a streamer. If you needed the 6X long for a big nymph there is still no problem, because even a little experience will tell you that a streamer hook is just a long nymph hook, more or less. The bottom line is this: First, hook choices are mostly subjective; second, hook manufacturers are not in all that much agreement anyway, so precise designations have varying meanings; and third, a bit of experience, or advice, and especially a glance at the hook or its picture will make the decision an easy one.

Finally, there are the hooks too odd to really fit into the system. Such hooks include "stinger," "caddis pupa," and "Swedish dry fly" types among others. Another way in which manufacturers create odd hooks is simply by giving them odd specifications. Perhaps there is something I am missing here, but isn't a hook designated as "wide gap" the same as a hook with a short shank? Odd hooks have their place, but most anglers still use conventional hooks, that *do* fit the system, the vast majority of the time.

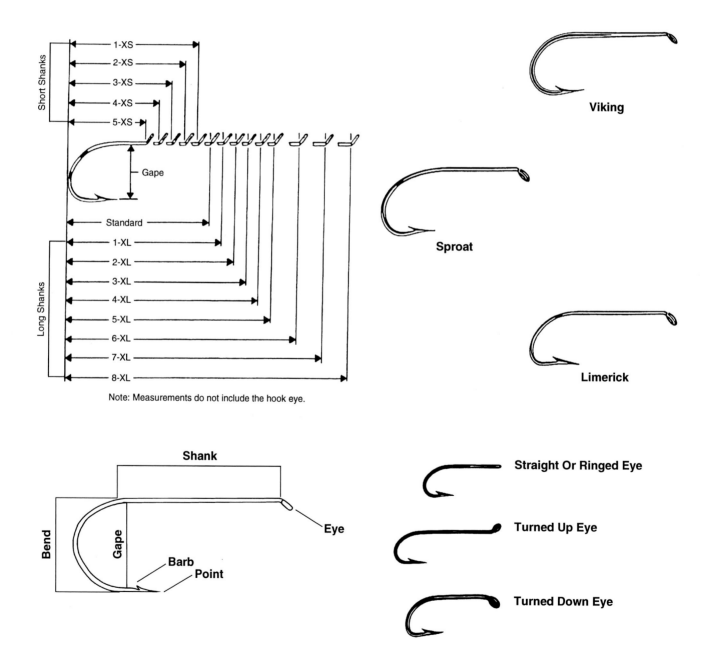

Note: Measurements do not include the hook eye.

Dry-Fly Hook Types

At one time, virtually all floating trout flies in America were tied on hooks made by the Mustad Company. Though a lot of flies are still tied on Mustad hooks, numerous other manufacturers now share the market.

Today's tier has a wider selection of hooks to choose from than ever before, but the problem is the added confusion. I don't claim to be familiar with every dry-fly hook available, but I've fished a lot of different hooks from a lot of different companies and I've done some homework. Here are the results:

Standard Dry Fly, Down Eye

Standard length, light wire, and an upturned eye is the traditional choice for a dry-fly hook, and it's still a good choice. Some anglers now prefer up eyes and ring eyes for dry flies—good-natured questioning of tradition keeps fly tying and fly fishing vital. I suggest you start with the traditional, and later explore your options.

Mustad 94840; Dai-Riki 305; Tiemco 5210, 100 (see "Wide Gape-Short Shank"); Partridge GRS 3A, L3A; Gamakatsu F-13; Daiichi 1170, 1180 ("mini-barb"; see "Standard Dry Fly, Barbless"); Eagle Claw D59.

Standard Dry Fly, Up Eye

Mustad 94842; Partridge L3B; Gamakatsu F-21; Eagle Claw D159.

Standard Dry Fly, Ring Eye

Mustad 94859; Dai-Riki 310; Tiemco 101 (see "Wide Gape-Short Shank"); Gamakatsu F-31; Orvis 1637.

Standard Dry Fly, Barbless

(up, down, or ring eye)

Most of the fly tiers I know smash the barbs on their hooks; this leaves a hump to do the barb's job of locking into a trout's mouth. Smashing barbs helps minimize the damage a hook might do to a fish that is released. A truly barbless hook, however—no barb, not even a hump—may even further reduce the risk of harming fish.

Mustad 94845; Tiemco 900BL; Partridge L3AY, CS20 (unusual "arrow point"); Gamakatsu F-11-B; Daiichi 1190, 1180 ("mini barb"; see also "Standard Dry Fly, Down Eye") 1480 ("mini-barb"; see "Wide Gape-Short Shank"); Eagle Claw D61B; Orvis 1877.

Long-Shank Dry Fly

(up, down, or ring eye)

Because several companies describe their long-shank dry-fly hooks as "hopper" hooks, "large dry fly" hooks and the like, I have included all long-shank hooks under this one heading—comparing shank lengths with descriptions like these just gets too ambiguous. For hooks from companies that sidestep the rules, your best solution is to judge a hook in question by looking at it, or a photograph or drawing of it.

Long-shank hooks can be perfect for imitations of stoneflies, grasshoppers, big mayflies, and many long-bodied or big insects. The relatively new humped-shank dry-fly hooks work; I'm experimenting with them and I suggest you do the same.

Mustad 94831; Dai-Riki 300; Tiemco 5212 (see "Extra Fine Wire"), 2302 (humped shank), 2312 (humped shank), 200R (humped shank); Partridge E1A, AFY (see "Wide Gape-Short Shank"; Gamakatsu F-14; Daiichi 1270 (humped shank); Orvis 1638, 1640 (humped shank).

Wide Gape-Short Shank Dry Fly

(up, down, or ring eye)

The terms "wide gape" and "short shank" are treated as interchangeable by most hook companies. Just what these terms mean is a bit vague—is a regular-shank, wide-gape hook the same as a hook with a 1X-short shank? I honestly don't know. The best answer is to look at a hook in question, or a photograph or drawing of it, and decide if the shank seems about right for your needs.

For tiny flies, a short shank means more gape and a bigger bite than a standard-length shank. For flies with a body that projects beyond the hook ("extended body"), a short shank means less iron, more buoyancy.

Mustad 94838; Tiemco 102Y, 500U, 501, 100 (see "Standard Dry Fly, Down Eye"), 101 (see "Standard Dry Fly, Ring Eye") 2487 (quite humped), 900BL (see "Barbless"); Partridge E6A, K1A, B, AFY (see "Barbless"); Daiichi 1640, 1330, 1480 (see "Barbless"), 1130 (quite humped); Orvis 1509, 1635, 4641 (large eye).

Extra-Fine-Wire Dry Fly

(up, down, or ring eye)

The finer the wire, the lighter the hook: That's the point behind extra-fine wire. After all, we are speaking here of hooks for flies that float. But finer wire also means a weaker hook, so weight has to be balanced against strength—if your Comparadun floats long and high, that will be small consolation when its hook gives under the run of a heavy rainbow.

Most dry-fly hooks have wire that is 1X fine; if extra strength is required, which is often the case with big fish, tiny flies, or both, a standard wire hook is used. Extra-fine wire is the stuff for dry flies with little to keep them afloat, such as the Antron Caddis and No Hackle. But even here, strength may still take precedence over buoyancy.

Mustad 94833; Tiemco 5230; Partridge L4A; Orvis 1523.

Heavy Wire Dry Fly

For big fish, especially in heavy water or where there are plenty of snags, heavy wire dry-fly hooks may be a necessity.

Tiemco 9300, 200R (see "Long Shank"); Partridge A; Daiichi 1480 (see "Long-Shank Dry Fly"); Orvis 1876.

XV

SENSIBLE FLY DESIGN

In high-school biology class I was taught that a scientist makes a hypothesis and objectively tests to prove or disprove it. The hypothesis is only the beginning of the process, testing is the bottom line, and objectivity makes the testing valid. Too many flies are designed by hypothesis only—these materials in this arrangement make sense, thinks the tier, and thus another fly pattern is born. What's missing is the other two-thirds of the process: testing and objectivity. I suspect that the problem with applying this to fly patterns is that a good idea sometimes seems too precious to be exposed to merciless truth. But the truth regarding a fly pattern's worth comes from testing and objectivity. A good fly designer has a lot in common with a scientist.

Testing teaches. And amid all the valuable truths and principles to be learned from testing fly patterns, these universal rules eventually stand out: Fragile materials must be reinforced or protected, fragile materials must not be secured at both ends and exposed between those ends, slippery materials must be tied in tightly over a long area or reinforced with glue, slippery materials shouldn't be wrapped over a steep taper, a fly pattern should be reasonably quick and easy to execute, and fly patterns should include only reasonably obtainable materials.

Let's examine these rules as they apply to real patterns. Consider the first rule concerning fragile materials; note how fragile

peacock herl and its stripped quill are reinforced with thread and glue in the H and L Variant—a sound approach which really enhances durability. The second rule states that fragile materials shouldn't be secured at both ends and exposed between—the deer-hair back of a Humpy is secured at both ends, but is deer hair fragile? Some is, some isn't; that's why tiers have always looked for the toughest deer hair for tying Humpies. The growing use of thick, durable elk hair for Humpies is surely a response to this principle. The H and L Variant is a good example of the slippery materials-long, tight tie-in rule—the calf-tail wings and tail of the H and L Variant are secured with tight thread wraps over most of the hook's shank.

By now you probably have the idea, but I'll fire off a few more quick examples. The slippery materials-steep taper rule—the Ginger Quill's slippery peacock-herl quill body is wrapped over an underbody of long, gradual taper. The easy-and-quick-to-tie rule—all my patterns and the logical, simple method for creating a reverse-wound hackle in the Elk Hair Caddis. The reasonably-obtainable-materials rule—nearly every fly in this book.

Exceptions? They're here too—no rule should be absolute. The Bunse Dun breaks two rules: the easy-and-quick-to-tie rule and the reasonably obtainable-materials rule. The Bunse Dun is slow to tie, and finding the ethafoam from

which it is made can require some hunting. But there are benefits to balance the breaking of these rules: The Bunse Dun has a natural, flexible upturned abdomen, and the ethafoam is buoyant and durable. To many anglers, these benefits outweigh the drawbacks.

The slippery materials-long, tight tie in rule would have the hackle-fiber tail of the Rat-Faced McDougal tied in at least halfway up the shank, but I need a bare shank in order to build a dense hair body, so I tie in the tail over just enough shank to do the job. So there are exceptions to the rules, but to make an exception justifiable there must be a significant payoff.

Virtually every fly tier will sooner or later experiment with original fly patterns, or at least variations of existing patterns—the draw to do so is almost irresistible. And that's part of the fun. Tie an Elk Hair Caddis with a peacock-herl body or a Rat-Faced McDougal with poly-yarn wings or take an idea or two from both patterns and create a new one. Most tiers tie and fish proven, established fly patterns and supplement these with variations and sometimes original patterns of their own. So the value of this book is that it provides the flies to round out a sound selection, and provides a foundation for variation, experimentation, and flights of fancy. But if you do experiment with fly patterns, experiment as a scientist would—with hypothesis, testing, and objectivity.

XVI

TRENDS IN
DRY-FLY DESIGN

It's easy to see where the dry fly has been; just read the works of Halford, Flick, Swisher and Richards, and others of such prominence and look at their flies. I am no fly-fishing historian, but as a teenager I recall thinking how similar the dry flies of Englishman Fredrick M. Halford, who wrote around the beginning of the nine-teen-hundreds, were to those in Art Flick's *Streamside Guide* published in 1947. This suggests that the essential form of the dry fly—wings set in a full hackle collar followed by a body and tail—changed little over a span of at least 30 years.

The real point here is where the dry fly is going. Of course things are never black and white; diverse and contrary paths all have their followers; one tier hoists the mayfly imitation above the surface on hackles for a natural posture while another tier condemns hackles as unnatural and too bushy to simulate insect legs and does away with them altogether. To identify the strongest trends one must step back, gain perspective.

Perhaps the strongest trend I have seen is towards effectiveness as the measure of a fly pattern's worth—if it fools fish, a pattern has merit. Consider the immense popularity of the Royal Coachman when I started fly fishing in the early 1960s. Here was a fly that had little to suggest a trout-food insect, but whose elegant title and appearance consis-

tently charmed fly fishers. A decade or so later, the somber Adams became the favored fly because it caught trout and looked "buggy." Today such unconventional, practical flies as the Elk Hair Caddis and Comparadun vie for the Adams's leading position. The Comparadun is a particularly good example of the effectiveness-worth principle—this fly looks odd indeed from the angler's perspective, but the trout have proven it out, and that is enough.

Synthetic materials are on the rise in all aspects of fly tying. To the dry-fly tier they offer durability, consistency, and buoyancy. Despite the occasional dogmatic cry for purity—that natural and synthetic materials should never meet on a fly hook, for what reason I can't possibly imagine—more and more patterns are surfacing that incorporate natural and synthetic materials, each doing what it does best. Examples are endless: the poly-yarn wing and parachute hackle of the Dark Green Drake, the macrame-yarn body and deer-hair head of the Matt's Adult Stone, the use of poly and antron dubbing in all types of traditional patterns. I suspect that we will see more foam, synthetic yarns, and synthetic braids used in dry flies. Realistic synthetic wing materials have drifted in and out of fly tying over the last decade, but I think that these too will take hold.

Though not really new, efforts to imitate insect stages other than the freshly hatched

adult are rapidly growing. The reason is that observation is revealing just how often partially hatched insects capture trout's attention. So we will see more patterns with names that include words like "emerging," "struggling," and "stillborn," and these patterns will mimic what those words suggest. This kind of thing blurs the line between patterns that was once so clear—is a floating nymph a nymph or a dry fly? But this line is a small and abstract issue, and exploring the many forms of trout insects is a sound and worthwhile pursuit.

That is about as clear as my crystal ball gets. There will surely be unexpected twists and innovations popping up. Indeed there have been many major trends in dry-fly design and lesser trends within the major. Some of these lesser trends have been only variations of the major trends, slight offshoots; others have been radical, even in direct, open conflict with the major trends. Since Halford, the dry fly has become slimmer and stouter, sparser and bushier, and has learned to ride higher and to squat down into and even almost completely under the water's surface. I wonder what Halford would think if he could come back today and see where his labors have led.

XVII

ADDITIONAL DRY FLIES

Mayfly Imitations:

1. ADAMS PARACHUTE

HOOK: Standard dry fly, sizes 18 to 10.
THREAD: Black or gray 8/0 or 6/0.
WING: White calf tail or calf body.
HACKLE: One grizzly and one brown mixed.
TAIL: Grizzly and brown hackle fibers mixed, or moose body.
BODY: Muskrat fur, dubbed.

COMMENTS: A version of the Adams that is steadily increasing in popularity. The hackles are wrapped one at a time; leave spaces in the turns of the first hackle and fill them with the second.

2. CDC RUSTY SPINNER
The Harrops

HOOK: Standard dry fly or extra-fine wire, sizes 24 to 12.
THREAD: Orange 8/0 or 6/0.
WING: White C D C feathers.
ABDOMEN: Rusty brown goose biot.
OVER WING: Light dun Z-lon.
THORAX: Rusty brown rabbit, dubbed.

COMMENTS: The technique for creating this wing is outlined under "The Poly Wing Spinner and CDC-Wing Spinner." The abdomen is formed by tying in a goose biot by its tip, clamping hackle pliers to the very end of its butt, and then wrapping it forward about two-thirds up the shank.

3. CDC TRANSITIONAL DUN
the Harrops

HOOK: Wide-gape dry fly, size to imitate any mayfly.
THREAD: 8/0 or 6/0, color to match thorax.
TAIL: Three or four wood-duck fibers or other fibers that match the natural, two shank lengths. Projecting over the tails, a tuft of dubbing, usually hare's mask.
ABDOMEN: Usually hare's mask, of a color to match the natural nymph, one half shank.
THORAX: Any dry-fly dubbing to match the color of the natural ;2dun.;1 Build a small collar to support the wings.
WINGS: Two CDC feather tips set back to back curving away from one another; color should match the natural (usually gray); length is 3/4 hook shank. The wings should sit up at 45 degrees.
LEGS: Butts of CDC feathers set to the sides and slanting back slightly, 3/4 shank length.

COMMENTS: The rear half of the Transitional Dun is a nymph and the front half is a hatching dun—a half-hatched mayfly. Great idea.

4. GREEN DRAKE PARADRAKE

HOOK: Standard dry fly, sizes 12 and 10.
THREAD: Yellow 3/0.
WING: Dyed gray elk hair.
TAIL: Moose-body hair.
BODY: Dyed olive elk hair.
HACKLE: Grizzly dyed yellow-olive.

COMMENTS: Tied in exactly the same manner as is the Brown Drake Paradrake.

5. HAIR WING SPINNER
Poul Jorgensen

HOOK: Standard dry fly, sizes 20 to 10 (Poul prefers an up-eye hook).
THREAD: Color to match body, 8/0 or 6/0.
WINGS: Deer hair.
TAILS: Hackle fibers, split.
ABDOMEN AND THORAX: Dubbing to match natural.

6. HEXAGENIA PARADRAKE

HOOK: Standard dry fly, sizes 10 to 6.
THREAD: Yellow 3/0.
WING: Dyed gray or yellow elk hair.
TAIL: Yellow elk hair.
BODY: Yellow elk hair.
HACKLE: Grizzly dyed yellow.

COMMENTS: *Hexagenia* is a huge yellow mayfly that hatches at twilight in lakes and quiet streams across America. When I first asked a friend about this hatch I said, "Do the trout really go after it?" He said, "*Everything* goes after the hex hatch." He went on to describe how trout, bass, panfish, and birds all feed in a frenzy when *Hexagenias* are popping. I've only fished hexes to trout, but they *were* frenzied trout.

7. IWAMASA DUN
Ken Iwamasa

HOOK: Standard or extra-light-wire dry fly, sizes 18 to 12.
THREAD: Color to match body in 8/0 or 6/0.
LEGS: Elk or deer hair.
THORAX: Dubbing, color to match natural.
TAILS: Moose-body hairs.
OVER BODY AND EXTENSION: Elk or deer hair.
WINGS: Hen saddle shaped in a wing burner.

COMMENTS: Tie in the legs, dub the shank, tie in the over body with the hairs' tips forward, tie in the tail fibers with points back, rib the thread down and up the body and extension, trim the extension leaving the tails, burn and add the wings. A simpler version of this pattern incorporates only a dubbed body and hackle-fiber tails. Iwamasa Duns are slow to tie, but some keen anglers swear by them.

8. LIGHT CAHILL PARACHUTE

HOOK: Standard dry fly, sizes 18 to 10.
THREAD: Tan 8/0 or 6/0.
WING: White calf tail.
HACKLE: Ginger.
TAIL: Ginger hackle fibers.
BODY: Badger underfur.

COMMENTS: A pale mayfly imitation.

9. MARCH BROWN COMPARADUN
Caucci and Nastasi

HOOK: Standard dry fly or extra-light wire, sizes 16 to 12.
THREAD: Tan 8/0, 6/0, or 3/0.
WING: Tan deer hair.
TAIL: Tan hackle fibers, split.
BODY: Tan dubbing.

COMMENTS: The western march brown begins its hatching as early as late winter. To some anglers it is the true start of the season. Recently I spent a day fishing this hatch with Richard Bunse, Deke Meyer, and Dave Hughes. Fishing with three of the sharpest fly fishers in the West, all better anglers than I, gave me occasional twinges of intimidation, but the payoff was a still, warm day of march browns and willing trout.

10. MAYFLY CRIPPLE
Bob Quigley

HOOK: Standard dry fly, size to match natural.
THREAD: Tan or a color appropriate to the natural in 8/0 or 6/0.
TAIL: Tan or olive-brown marabou, slightly short.
BODY: Stripped light-brown hackle stem.
THORAX: Tan poly dubbing or a color to match the natural.
WING: Tan deer or elk hair. The tips project over the eye and the butts are trimmed close over the thorax.
HACKLE: Three to five turns of light ginger or appropriate color.

COMMENTS: This suggests a mayfly trapped halfway out of its shuck.

11. MORRIS MAY DARK
Skip Morris

HOOK: Standard dry fly, sizes 24 to 10.
THREAD: Brown 3/0.
TAIL: Brown hackle fibers, split.
BODY: Brown poly dubbing.
WING: Gray poly yarn.
HACKLE: Brown, one, palmered over the thorax and trimmed beneath.

COMMENTS: For over a decade the Morris May was my standard mayfly imitation, but some of the latest variations of the Thorax Dun are nearly indistinguishable from it. Try both the light and dark versions in appropriate size to match all types of mayflies.

ADAMS PARACHUTE   CDC RUSTY SPINNER   CDC TRANSITIONAL DUN

GREEN DRAKE PARADRAKE   HAIR WING SPINNER   HEXAGENIA PARADRAKE

IWAMASA DUN   LIGHT CAHILL PARACHUTE   MARCH BROWN COMPARADUN

MAYFLY CRIPPLE   MORRIS MAY DARK

ADDITIONAL DRY FLIES   99

12. MORRIS MAY LIGHT
Skip Morris

HOOK: Standard dry fly, sizes 24 to 10.
THREAD: Tan 8/0 or 6/0.
TAIL: Ginger hackle fibers, split.
BODY: Tan poly dubbing.
WING: Gray poly yarn.
HACKLE: Ginger, one, palmered over the thorax and trimmed beneath.

13. NO HACKLE
Swisher and Richards

HOOK: Standard or extra-fine wire dry fly, sizes 22 to 12.
THREAD: Color to match thorax, 8/0 or 6/0.
TAIL: Hackle fibers, split, color to match natural.
ABDOMEN: Dubbing of color to match natural.
WINGS: Duck-quill sections tied in with their butts forward. Dubbed thread is criss-crossed between the wings.
THORAX: Dubbing of a color to match abdomen.

COMMENTS: There are many specific color schemes for No Hackles: Gray/Yellow (gray wing and yellow body), Gray/Olive, etc. The pattern listed here is general, allowing for many combinations. The No Hackle was revolutionary when it first appeared nearly 20 years ago; it remains popular today.

14. NO-HACKLE STILLBORN
Swisher and Richards

HOOK: Standard or extra-fine-wire dry fly, sizes 22 to 12.
THREAD: Color to match thorax, 8/0 or 6/0.
SHUCK: Hen hackle trimmed to shape (light to dark depending on natural).
ABDOMEN: Dubbing of a color to match the natural.
WINGS: Duck-quill sections.
THORAX: Dubbing of color to match abdomen.

COMMENTS: There are lots of Swisher-Richards stillborn variations—hair shuck, poly-yarn shuck, hackle-tip wings, duck-shoulder wings—but this no-hackle version is as established as any. The principle here is the same one behind the Sparkle Dun and the CDC Transitional Dun.

15. PALE MORNING DUN THORAX

HOOK: Standard dry fly, sizes 18 and 16.
THREAD: Yellow 8/0 or 6/0.
WING: Gray turkey flats or substitute.
TAIL: Blue dun hackle fibers, split.
BODY: Yellow dubbing.
HACKLE: One, blue dun.

COMMENTS: Pale morning duns are western mayflies that hatch over a long stretch of the fishing season. If you fish western streams, be prepared for the pale morning dun hatch.

16. TWO FEATHER FLY
Harry and Elsie Darbee

HOOK: Short shank, dry fly (Harry only describes the fly on a size 16 hook, but surely other sizes would work).
THREAD: 8/0 or 6/0 color to match the body-wing feather.
BODY: Spade hackle or other feather stroked and coated with Pliobond.
WINGS: Tips of body feather.
HACKLE: One of a color to match natural.

COMMENTS: Quite a concept. A feather is stripped of fibers at its butt, all but the tip of the feather is stroked forward and tied in, the center is snipped from the tip, the extension is coated with Pliobond, the tips of the fibers are divided into wings, the hackle is tied in and wound. A very light fly on a small hook.

17. UNFINISHED SPINNER
Vincent Marinaro

HOOK: Standard dry fly (as far as I know, Marinaro never mentioned hook size for this fly).
THREAD: Color to match the body, 8/0 or 6/0.
WINGS: A dry fly hackle wound forward and then back to flare it. The hackle is then gathered into wings with crisscrossed thread turns.
TAILS: Hackle fibers, color to match natural.
BODY: Dubbing to match natural (Marinaro preferred seal's fur twisted on a dubbing loop and trimmed).

COMMENTS: Vince Marinaro was a bit vague about the details of his Unfinished Spinner, but he was clear about its wing construction and the theory behind it. The Unfinished Spinner was described in his book *In The Ring Of The Rise*. Most tiers will probably use a different dubbing material than seal and forego the dubbing loop.

18. YARN WING DUN
Gary Borger

HOOK: Standard dry fly, sizes 16 to 6.
THREAD: Color to match body, 8/0 or 6/0.
TAIL: Hackle fibers tied in fan style (my split-tail method without trimming out the center), color to match body.
BODY: Dubbing to match natural.
HACKLE: One hackle spiraled forward from midshank, spiraled back, and then forward again to splay the fibers. Trim the fibers away beneath the body. Color should match the wing.
WING: Poly yarn tied in just behind eye and trimmed (much like the method used for the Elk Hair Caddis wing).

COMMENTS: Another approach to the mayfly-imitation challenge.

Caddisfly Imitations

1. BLACK ELK HAIR CADDIS

HOOK: Standard dry fly, sizes 18 to 8.
THREAD: Black 3/0.
RIB: Fine gold wire.
BODY: Black dubbing.
HACKLE: Black.
WING: Elk hair dyed black.

COMMENTS: A logical, casually evolved variation of the Elk Hair Caddis that gets plenty of use.

2. DEER HAIR CADDIS
Jim Schollmeyer

HOOK: Standard dry fly, size 20 to 10.
THREAD: Gray 3/0.
HACKLE: Blue dun palmered up body and trimmed flat underneath in line with hook point.
BODY: Olive dubbing.
WING: Natural gray deer hair.

COMMENTS: Jim is reluctant to take credit for this pattern as it borrows so much from Al Troth's Elk Hair Caddis, but as far as Jim or I know, the first Deer Hair Caddis came from Jim's vise.

3. DELTA WING CADDIS
Larry Solomon

HOOK: Standard dry fly, sizes 22 to 10.
THREAD: Olive 8/0 or 6/0.
ABDOMEN: Light olive dubbing; other colors can be used.
WINGS: Gray hen-neck hackles tied spent and slanting slightly back.
HACKLE: Brown, fibers trimmed away underneath; other colors can be used.
THORAX: Light olive dubbing.

COMMENTS: Larry says that the Delta Wing Caddis suggests "an adult caddis that cannot quite extricate itself from its pupal overcoat, or a partially crippled insect of that species."

4. FALL CADDIS

HOOK: Long shank, dry fly, sizes 10 to 6.
THREAD: Black 3/0.
RIB: One brown hackle, slightly small, palmered.
BODY: Orange dubbing.
WING: Natural brown deer hair.
HACKLE: Brown, heavy.

COMMENTS: I found this pattern in *The Western Streamside Guide*, an excellent, straightforward western-insect-matching book by my friend Dave Hughes. Big and vigorous, the fall caddis stirs big western trout in September and October, but just fishing amid the fluttering brown and orange gives fall fishing a distinctive flavor.

5. FLAT WING CADDIS

HOOK: Standard dry fly, sizes 22 to 12.
THREAD: Brown 8/0 or 6/0.
ABDOMEN: Gray dubbing (other colors can be used).
RIB: One palmered brown hackle trimmed top and bottom.
WING: A partridge feather cemented, drawn between thumb and finger, and a notch trimmed in its end.
HACKLE: One brown hackle trimmed on the bottom (other colors can be used).

COMMENTS: This style produces a precise, durable wing silhouette.

MORRIS MAY LIGHT   NO HACKLE   NO-HACKLE STILLBORN

PALE MORNING DUN THORAX   TWO FEATHER FLY   UNFINISHED SPINNER

YARN WING DUN   BLACK ELK HAIR CADDIS   DEER HAIR CADDIS

DELTA WING CADDIS   FALL CADDIS   FLAT WING CADDIS

6. HEMMINGWAY CADDIS

HOOK: Standard dry fly, sizes 20 to 12.
THREAD: Olive 8/0 or 6/0.
RIB: One blue dun hackle palmered.
ABDOMEN: Olive dubbing.
UNDER WING: Wood-duck feather fibers.
WING: One duck-quill section rolled over the
    top of the thorax. The section is trimmed
    round on its tip.
THORAX: Peacock herl.
HACKLE: One blue dun hackle palmered over
    the thorax.

7. KINGS RIVER CADDIS

HOOK: Standard dry fly, sizes 18 to 12.
THREAD: Brown 8/0 or 6/0.
BODY: Tan dubbing.
WING: Mottled turkey-quill section pointed
    and notched.
HACKLE: Brown.

8. PARACHUTE CADDIS
Ed Schroeder

HOOK: Standard dry fly, sizes 18 to 10.
THREAD: Cream 8/0 or 6/0.
WING: White calf tail.
HACKLE: Grizzly, parachute.
ABDOMEN: Hare's mask fur, dubbed.
WING: Mottled turkey-quill section notched in
    end.
THORAX: Hare's mask fur, dubbed.

COMMENTS: The white upright wing provides visibility and a base for the parachute
hackle. This fly has passed a key test—it developed a considerable following quickly.

9. POLY CADDIS
Gary Borger

HOOK: Standard dry fly, sizes 24 to 8.
THREAD: Color to match the wing, 8/0 or
    6/0.
BODY: Dubbing of a color to match the
    natural.
HACKLE: One hackle spiraled forward, back,
    and forward (see the "Yarn Wing Dun"
    under "Mayfly Imitations" in this
    section). Trim the hackle beneath.
WING: Poly yarn of a color to match the
    natural. Trim the butts as a head.

10. SID NEFF HAIRWING
Sid Neff

HOOK: Standard dry fly, sizes 20 to 12.
THREAD: Brown 8/0, 6/0, or 3/0.
BODY: Brown-gray dubbing.
WING: Natural brown-gray deer hair.
HEAD: Butts of wing. The butts are trimmed,
    and then the thread is wound through
    them to set them upright.

11. SLOW WATER CADDIS
the Harrops

HOOK: Standard dry fly, sizes 20 to 12.
THREAD: Color to match body, 8/0 or 6/0.
BODY: Dubbing of a color to match the
    natural (Rene' prefers natural dubbings).
HACKLE: One, same color as the body. The
    hackle is tied in at midshank, palmered
    forward only a few turns, tied off, and
    then the dubbing is continued forward.
    Trim the hackle top and bottom.
UNDER WING: Elk or deer hair, sparse.
OVER WING: Two hen saddle hackles
    stiffened with Dave's Flexament.

12. SOLOMON'S HAIRWING
Larry Solomon

HOOK: Standard dry fly, sizes 22 to 8.
THREAD: Gray 8/0 or 6/0.
BODY: Light olive dubbing; other colors can
    be used.
WING: Deer hair tied in about two-thirds up
    the shank; light thread turns at front of
    body to gather wing.
HACKLE: One or two as desired, brown,
    wrapped over thorax.

COMMENTS: Larry adds a bit of head cement
to the wing thread wraps to secure them. I like
to wrap the hackle right after adding the
cement which then secures the hackle as well.

13. TAN ELK HAIR CADDIS

HOOK: Standard dry fly, sizes 18 to 8.
THREAD: Tan 3/0.
RIB: Fine gold wire.
BODY: Tan dubbing.
HACKLE: Ginger.
WING: Bleached elk hair.

COMMENTS: A generic, pale version of the
Elk Hair Caddis.

Stonefly Imitations

1. BIRD'S STONEFLY
Cal Bird

HOOK: Long shank, dry fly, sizes 14 to 4.
THREAD: Orange 3/0.
TAIL: Two moose-body hairs, split.
BODY: Alternate bands of orange floss and
    trimmed brown hackle.
WING: Dark buck tail or squirrel tail.
HACKLE: Brown; use plenty of hackle.
ANTENNAE: Two moose-body hairs, split.

2. DARK STONE
Polly Rosborough

HOOK: Long shank, dry fly, sizes 8 and 6.
THREAD: Black 3/0.
RIB: One palmered furnace hackle.
BODY: Orange yarn (or substitute dubbing).
WING: Brown buck tail.
HACKLE: Furnace; use plenty of hackle.

COMMENTS: The strong similarity of the
Dark Stone to the Fall Caddis illustrates a
point: From a trout's perspective, adult caddisflies and stoneflies look much the same. I consider these two patterns interchangeable.

3. FLUTTERING GOLDEN STONEFLY
Nevin Stephenson

HOOK: Standard dry fly (or heavy wire), sizes
8 and 6.
THREAD: Yellow 3/0.
BODY: Twisted yellow poly yarn (see "The
    Skipping Stone").
WING: Light natural elk hair.
HACKLE: Dark ginger, plenty of hackle.
ANTENNAE: Eight-pound test monofilament
    dyed gold (or substitute ginger hackle
    stems.)

4. HENRY'S FORK GOLDEN STONE
Mike Lawson

HOOK: Long shank, dry fly, sizes 10 to 6.
THREAD: Tan 3/0.
BODY: Elk hair dyed gold, drawn forward
    (see the section titled "The Henry's Fork
    Hopper").
WING: Natural brown elk hair.
HEAD AND COLLAR: Elk hair dyed gold
    (dyed-yellow or naturally light elk hair
    would be my choices as substitutes).

HEMMINGWAY CADDIS   KINGS RIVER CADDIS   PARACHUTE CADDIS

POLY CADDIS   SID NEFF HAIRWING   SLOW WATER CADDIS

SOLOMON'S HAIR WING   TAN ELK HAIR CADDIS   BIRD'S STONEFLY

DARK STONE   FLUTTERING GOLDEN STONEFLY   HENRY'S FORK GOLDEN STONE

ADDITIONAL DRY FLIES   103

5. IMPROVED SOFA PILLOW
Pat and Sig Barnes

HOOK: Long shank, dry fly, sizes 10 to 4.
THREAD: Black 3/0.
TAIL: Elk hair.
RIB: Palmered brown hackle.
BODY: Orange yarn or dubbing.
WING: Elk hair.
HACKLE: Brown; use plenty of hackle.

6. JUGHEAD
Betty Hoyt

HOOK: Long shank, dry fly, sizes 10 to 4.
THREAD: Black 3/0; Size-A rod-winding thread for the head.
TAIL: Elk Hair.
RIB: One palmered brown hackle with its fibers trimmed.
BODY: Orange poly yarn.
UNDER WING: Elk hair (optional).
WING: Red-fox squirrel tail.
HEAD: Natural deer hair spun and shaped.
COLLAR: (Optional) the tips of the head hair.

7. LANGTRY SPECIAL

HOOK: Long shank, dry fly, sizes 10 to 6.
THREAD: Orange 3/0.
TAIL: Natural tan elk hair.
RIB: Brown hackle, palmered over abdomen.
ABDOMEN: Cream dubbing.
WING: Natural tan elk hair.
HACKLE: Brown, palmered over thorax.
THORAX: Orange dubbing.

COMMENTS: A popular imitation of the western salmon fly.

8. MacSALMON
Al Troth

HOOK: Long shank, dry fly, sizes 8 to 2.
THREAD: Brown 3/0 (I use size-A rod-winding thread for the head and collar.
BODY: A section of orange polypropylene macrame yarn melted at the end (see "Matt's Adult Stone"). The hook's point is pushed partway down the yarn.
UNDER WING: Dark-gray synthetic wing material cut to shape (Al prefers Fly Sheet).
OVER WING: Pale elk hair.
HEAD AND COLLAR: Dark brown deer hair (Al trims the front of the head to a taper).

COMMENTS: Quite similar to the Matt's Adult Stone. I have one beautifully tied by Al and mounted behind glass.

9. SOFA PILLOW
Pat Barnes

HOOK: Long shank, dry fly, sizes 10 to 4.
THREAD: Black 3/0.
TAIL: A section of dyed-red duck quill.
BODY: Red floss.
WING: Red-fox squirrel tail.
HACKLE: Brown; use plenty of hackle.

COMMENTS: A proven old-time salmon-fly imitation.

Tiny Flies

1. BLACK MIDGE

HOOK: Standard dry fly, sizes 24 to 16.
THREAD: Black 8/0 or finer.
TAIL: Black hackle fibers.
BODY: Black thread or dubbing.
HACKLE: Black.

2. BLUE DUN MIDGE

HOOK: Standard dry fly, sizes 24 to 16.
THREAD: Gray 8/0 or finer.
TAIL: Blue-dun hackle fibers.
BODY: Muskrat fur dubbed or substitute.
HACKLE: Blue-dun.

3. CREAM MIDGE

HOOK: Standard dry fly, sizes 24 to 16.
THREAD: Cream 8/0 or finer.
TAIL: Cream hackle fibers.
BODY: Cream dubbing.
HACKLE: Cream.

4. GULPER SPECIAL
Al Troth

HOOK: Standard dry fly, sizes 18 to 24.
THREAD: Brown 8/0.
WING: White, black, or orange poly yarn (these are the colors Al uses to increase visibility).
HACKLE: Grizzly, parachute style.
TAIL: Grizzly hackle fibers.
BODY: Brown dubbing.

COMMENTS: Gulpers can be tied larger and in other shades to imitate other insects, but this version is used for imitating tiny *Tricorythodes* mayfly duns. Al ties in the wing with the rotated method described in "The Poly Wing Spinner and CDC-Wing Spinner."

5. JASSID
Vincent Marinaro

HOOK: Standard dry fly size 22, or short-shank dry fly size 20.
THREAD: Black 8/0.
RIB: Palmered black hackle trimmed below and on top.
BODY: None really, just the thread that secures the hackle.
WING: One jungle-cock nail, flat.

COMMENTS: The jungle-cock nail represents the outline of the jassid.

6. LITTLE OLIVE PARACHUTE

HOOK: Standard dry fly, sizes 22 to 16.
THREAD: Olive 8/0 or finer.
WING: White calf tail.
HACKLE: Blue-dun, parachute.
TAIL: Blue-dun hackle fibers, split.
BODY: Olive dubbing.

COMMENTS: An imitation of the tiny *Baetis* mayfly.

Terrestrial Imitations

1. BLACK CROWE BEETLE

HOOK: Standard dry fly, sizes 22 to 12.
THREAD: Black 8/0, 6/0, or 3/0 (I prefer the 3/0).
BACK: Dyed black deer or elk hair (I prefer elk).
LEGS: A few of the hair butts.

COMMENTS: Tie in the hairs in the shank's center, wrap the thread back to the bend and then forward to its starting point, trim away all but a few leg hairs, divide the leg hairs to the sides, advance the thread, pull down and secure the hair back, trim the hairs for a head and trim the leg hairs to length.

IMPROVED SOFA PILLOW   JUGHEAD   LANGTRY SPECIAL

MacSALMON   SOFA PILLOW   BLACK MIDGE

BLUE DUN MIDGE   CREAM MIDGE   GULPER SPECIAL

JASSID   LITTLE OLIVE PARACHUTE   BLACK CROWE BEETLE

2. BRIGHT SPOT CARPENTER ANT
Dave Whitlock

HOOK: Standard dry fly, extra light wire, sizes 16 to 8.
THREAD: Black 8/0 or 6/0.
BODY: Black moose-body or elk-body hair.
LEGS: Moose-body hairs.
BRIGHT SPOT: Fluorescent pink or orange deer hair tied in over the legs and trimmed closely.

COMMENTS: The rear body hair is tied in at the bend and pulled forward and trimmed; the front body hair is tied in behind the eye and then pulled back and trimmed. Add legs and pink or orange hair (although I'd choose yellow).

3. CALCATERRA ANT
Paul Calcaterra

HOOK: Standard dry fly, sizes 22 to 12.
THREAD: Black 8/0, 6/0, or 3/0 (I prefer the 3/0).
EVERYTHING ELSE: Dyed black deer hair (I prefer elk hair).

COMMENTS: The hair is tied in at the bend, pulled forward, a few hairs are snipped free at the bend to form legs, thread is advanced, hair is pulled forward and secured and trimmed. Add a coating of lacquer over the body sections.

4. INCHWORM

HOOK: Standard dry fly, sizes 16 to 12.
THREAD: Green 3/0.
BODY: Green deer or elk hair (I prefer elk).
RIB: Green 3/0.

COMMENTS: There seem to be as many ways to tie this fly as there are books to describe it; the hair can be tied in at the eye and pulled back, tied in at the bend and pulled forward, tied in and trimmed at both ends, extended, not extended. All will work; you decide.

5. JAPANESE BEETLE
Vincent Marinaro

HOOK: Standard dry fly, size 16.
THREAD: Black 8/0 or 6/0.
HACKLE: Two short-fibered black hackles palmered up thread base and around legs and trimmed away beneath and on top.
LEGS: Three black ostrich herls tied in criss crossing about two-thirds up the shank, cut to length. (I suspect that the fibers should be trimmed close.)
BACK (WING): A jungle-cock nail tied in flat over the shank.

6. JOE'S HOPPER

HOOK: Long shank, dry fly, sizes 12 to 6.
THREAD: Black 8/0, 6/0, or 3/0.
TAIL: Red hackle fibers.
RUMP: A loop of the body yarn over the tail.
RIB: Brown hackle palmered up the body and trimmed.
BODY: Yellow yarn (I prefer poly yarn).
WINGS: Turkey quill sections tied down-wing style with tips up.
HACKLE: Brown and grizzly mixed.

COMMENTS: An old-time hopper imitation.

7. MacHOPPER
Al Troth

HOOK: Long shank, dry fly, size 8.
THREAD: Yellow 3/0 (I use size-A rod-winding thread for the head and collar).
BODY: A section of yellow polypropelene macrame yarn melted at the end (see "The Matt's Adult Stone"). The hook's point is pushed partway down the yarn.
UNDER WING: Yellow synthetic wing material cut to shape.
OVER WING: Yellow elk or deer.
LEGS: Rubber strands (see "The Jay-Dave's Hopper").
HEAD AND COLLAR: Olive or olive-yellow deer hair.

Traditional Dry Flies

1. AMERICAN MARCH BROWN
Art Flick

HOOK: Standard dry fly, sizes 12 and 10.
THREAD: Orange 8/0 or 6/0.
WINGS: Mandarin-drake flank feather sections (or substitute bronze mallard or well-marked wood duck).
TAIL: Ginger hackle fibers.
BODY: Red-fox fur, dubbed (or any beige dubbing).
HACKLE: Ginger grizzly (or regular ginger) and grizzly mixed.

COMMENTS: This is Art Flick's version of Preston Jennings's original. The American March Brown imitates an eastern mayfly of the same name.

2. BADGER SPIDER

HOOK: Short shank, dry fly, sizes 16 and 14.
THREAD: Black 8/0 or 6/0.
TAIL: Badger hackle fibers, long.
BODY: (Optional) flat silver tinsel.
HACKLE: Badger, oversize.

COMMENTS: Though similar to variants, spiders always lack wings and seem to imitate anything or nothing; obviously they *can* be used to imitate real spiders.

3. BLACK GNAT

HOOK: Standard dry fly, sizes 18 to 12.
THREAD: Black 6/0 or 8/0.
WING: Duck-quill sections.
TAIL: Black hackle fibers.
BODY: Black dubbing (many tiers used to use chenille, but it is too absorbent).
HACKLE: Black.

4. BLUE DUN

HOOK: Standard dry fly, sizes 18 to 12.
THREAD: Gray 6/0 or 8/0.
WINGS: Duck-quill sections.
TAIL: Blue-dun hackle fibers.
BODY: Muskrat fur, dubbed.
HACKLE: Blue dun.

5. BROWN BIVISIBLE

HOOK: Standard dry fly, sizes 16 to 10.
THREAD: Black 8/0 or 6/0.
TAIL: Brown hackle fibers (optional).
HACKLE: Three or more hackles over most of the shank with a few turns of white in front.

COMMENTS: "Bivisible" is meant to indicate that the fly is visible to both angler and trout—white hackle for the angler, dark for the trout. There are all kinds of Bivisibles—blue dun, grizzly, badger. These were popular for their visibility, buoyancy, and because they suggest many kinds of insects.

6. CREAM VARIANT
Art Flick

HOOK: Short shank, dry fly, size 12.
THREAD: Yellow 8/0 or 6/0.
WING: None.
TAIL: Cream hackle fibers, long.
BODY: Cream hackle stem.
HACKLE: Oversize cream.

COMMENTS: Like most flies called variants, the tails and hackles are oversize. The Cream Variant imitates an eastern mayfly.

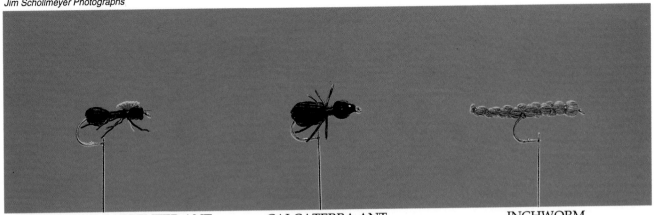

BRIGHT SPOT CARPENTER ANT　　　CALCATERRA ANT　　　INCHWORM

JAPANESSE BEETLE　　　JOE'S HOPPER　　　MacHOPPER

AMERICAN MARCH BROWN　　　BADGER SPIDER　　　BLACK GNAT

BLUE DUN　　　BROWN BIVISIBLE　　　CREAM VARIANT

7. DELAWARE ADAMS
Walt Dette

HOOK: Standard dry fly, sizes 16 to 10.
THREAD: White 8/0 or 6/0.
WINGS: Grizzly hackle tips.
TAIL: Grizzly hackle fibers.
RIB: Grizzly hackle, palmered.
BODY: Green dubbing.
HACKLE: Grizzly and brown, mixed.

8. GREY FOX
Preston Jennings

HOOK: Standard dry fly, size 12.
THREAD: Primrose 8/0 or 6/0 ("primrose" can mean light yellow or pink; it seems likely that Jennings was referring to pink).
WINGS: Mallard flank.
TAIL: Ginger hackle fibers.
BODY: Light red-fox fur.
HACKLE: Ginger and grizzly mixed.

COMMENTS: The Grey Fox imitates the eastern mayfly *Stenonema vicarium*.

9. HENDRICKSON
Roy Steenrod

HOOK: Standard dry fly, size 12.
THREAD: Gray 8/0 or 6/0.
WINGS: Wood-duck fibers.
TAIL: Blue-dun hackle fibers.
BODY: Pink red-fox fur (or any dubbing of a pink cast).
HACKLE: Blue dun.

COMMENTS: Imitates the hendrickson mayfly.

10. QUILL GORDON
Theodore Gordon

HOOK: Standard dry fly, sizes 14 and 16.
THREAD: Gray 8/0 or 6/0.
WINGS: Wood duck.
TAIL: Blue-dun hackle fibers.
BODY: Stripped peacock quill.
HACKLE: Blue dun.

11. RED QUILL
Art Flick

HOOK: Standard dry fly, sizes 18 to 12.
THREAD: Black 8/0 or 6/0.
WINGS: Wood duck.
TAIL: Blue-dun hackle fibers.
BODY: Stripped quill from reddish-brown dry-fly hackle.
HACKLE: Blue dun.

COMMENTS: The Red Quill was intended as an imitation of the male hendickson mayfly, but anglers use it for all sorts of duty.

12. ROYAL COACHMAN

HOOK: Standard dry fly, sizes 20 to 10.
THREAD: Black 8/0 or 6/0.
WINGS: White duck-quill sections.
TAIL: Golden pheasant tippets.
BODY: Rear third is peacock herl; center is red floss; front third is herl again.
HACKLE: Brown.

COMMENTS: Though still popular, the Royal Coachman was once *terribly* popular, and from that popularity came many variations—Royal Coachman Bucktail, Royal Wulff, Royal Trude. The Royal Coachman imitates nothing, but it's caught a tremendous number of trout over the years.

Rough-Water Flies

1. ADAMS IRRESISTIBLE

HOOK: Standard dry fly, sizes 16 to 10.
THREAD: Gray 8/0, 6/0, or 3/0; size-A rod-winding thread for spinning the body hair.
TAIL: Brown and grizzly hackle fibers mixed.
BODY: Spun and shaped deer or caribou hair.
WINGS: Grizzly hackle tips.
HACKLE: Brown and grizzly mixed.

2. GRAY WULFF
Lee Wulff

HOOK: Standard dry fly, sizes 16 to 8.
THREAD: Gray 6/0, 8/0, or 3/0.
WINGS: Brown bucktail or substitute.
TAIL: Brown bucktail or substitute.
BODY: Gray yarn or dubbing.
HACKLE: Blue dun; use plenty of hackle.

3. GRIZZLY WULFF
Lee Wulff

HOOK: Standard dry fly, sizes 16 to 8.
THREAD: Black 8/0, 6/0, or 3/0.
WINGS: Brown buck tail or substitute.
TAIL: Brown buck tail or substitute.
BODY: Yellow floss or substitute yellow dubbing.
HACKLE: Brown and grizzly mixed; use plenty of hackle.

4. IRRESISTIBLE

HOOK: Standard dry fly, sizes 16 to 8.
THREAD: Gray or black 8/0, 6/0, or 3/0; size-A rod-winding thread for spinning the hair.
TAIL: Brown bucktail.
BODY: Deer or caribou hair spun and shaped.
WINGS: Brown bucktail.
HACKLE: Blue dun; use plenty of hackle.

5. IRRESISTIBLE WULFF

HOOK: Standard dry fly, sizes 16 to 8.
THREAD: Black 8/0, 6/0, or 3/0; size-A rod-winding thread for spinning the hair.
TAIL: Moose-body hair.
BODY: Deer or caribou hair spun and shaped.
WINGS: White calf tail.
HACKLE: Brown; use plenty of hackle.

6. ROYAL COACHMAN TRUDE
Carter Harrison

HOOK: Standard dry fly, sizes 16 to 8.
THREAD: Black 3/0, 6/0, or 8/0.
TAIL: Golden pheasant tippets.
BODY: Peacock herl, red floss, herl (see the Royal Coachman pattern in this section under "Traditional Dry Flies").
WING: White calf tail tied down-wing style.
HACKLE: Brown; use plenty of hackle.

COMMENENTS: Another variation of the once terribly popular Royal Coachman.

DELAWARE ADAMS   GREY FOX   HENDRICKSON

QUILL GORDON   RED QUILL   ROYAL COACHMAN

ADAMS IRRESISTABLE   GRAY WULFF   GRIZZLY WULFF

IRRESISTIBLE   IRRESISTIBLE WULFF   ROYAL COACHMAN TRUDE

7. ROYAL HUMPY

HOOK: Standard dry fly, sizes 16 to 8.
THREAD: Red 3/0 or single-strand floss.
TAIL: Moose body.
HUMP: Elk or moose-body hair.
BODY: Red thread or single-strand floss.
WINGS: White calf tail; the wings are tied in after the hump is formed and trimmed.
HACKLE: Brown.

COMMENTS: Another Royal Coachman variation, but this one is particularly visible for its white wings. For tying instructions see "The Humpy" in section VII, "Rough-Water Flies."

8. WHITE WULFF
Lee Wulff

HOOK: Standard dry fly, sizes 16 to 8.
THREAD: Black 8/0, 6/0, or 3/0.
WINGS: White calf tail.
TAIL: White calf tail.
BODY: Cream yarn or substitute cream wool.
HACKLE: Pale badger.

Miscellaneous Dry Flies

1. BRAIDED BUTT DAMSEL
Gary Borger

HOOK: Standard dry fly, sizes 12 and 10.
THREAD: Black 8/0 or 6/0.
ABDOMEN: Braided leader, melted at the end to hold the braid, and colored with marking pens; colors include olive, and light blue with black marks at intervals.
BACK-HACKLE POST: Blue poly yarn for the blue abdomen and olive for the olive.
HACKLE: Blue dun, parachute style.
THORAX: Dubbing to match the abdomen's color.

COMMENTS: After the parachute hackle is wrapped and secured, its fibers are stroked back, the yarn is pulled forward and secured, and the yarn is trimmed. The hackle fibers create wings.

2. CLARK'S DAMSELFLY
Lee Clark

HOOK: Long shank, dry fly, size 12 and 10.
THREAD: Black 8/0 or 6/0.
BODY: Bright metallic-blue mylar cut from a potato-chip bag (I've found a similar color in Flashabou).
OVER BODY: Light-blue poly yarn, twisted.
WING: Dyed black deer hair, down-wing style.
HACKLE: Black.
HEAD: Cut ends of the poly-yarn over body.

3. CLUMPER MIDGE
Si Upson

HOOK: Standard dry fly, size 14.
THREAD: Black 6/0 or 8/0.
WING: A short tuft of black poly yarn flared by tight thread wraps at its base.
HACKLE: Black, parachute style.
TAIL: Two moose-body hairs, split.
BODY: Black poly yarn.

COMMENTS: Clumps of midges tend to form around mating time ; the Clumper Midge suggests such an amorous clump.

4. MADAM X
Doug Swisher

HOOK: Long shank, dry fly, sizes 8 and 6.
THREAD: Yellow 3/0.
BODY AND TAIL: Natural deer hair tied in well up shank; thread is spiraled down the body and back up.
HEAD AND WING: Deer hair tied in behind eye and pulled up and back and then secured with a thread collar (the hair should stay on top, not radiate like a regular bullet head).
LEGS: Yellow round rubber legs, one section on each side tied in at the collar.

COMMENTS: A true western attractor pattern, though some use it as a stonefly imitation.

5. MUDDLER (Dry)

HOOK: Long shank, dry fly, size 14 to 8.
THREAD: Yellow 3/0, size-A rod-winding thread for the head.
TAIL: Brown mottled turkey-quill section.
BODY: Yellow poly yarn.
UNDER WING: White calf tail.
WINGS: Brown mottled turkey-quill sections.
HEAD AND COLLAR: Deer hair.

COMMENTS: Originally a popular imitation of a "sculpin," a small fish. Before Muddler Minnows soaked up enough water to sink, trout were taking them on top; thus the dry version.

6. RENEGADE

HOOK: Standard dry fly, size 18 to 10.
THREAD: Black 8/0 or 6/0.
REAR HACKLE: Brown, slightly small.
BODY: Peacock herl.
FRONT HACKLE: White.

COMMENTS: Though it has been around for a long time, compared with most dry flies this pattern is still a renegade. The Renegade is truly an attractor fly; it imitates nothing more specific than a plump, floating insect.

7. WATERWALKER
Frank Johnson

HOOK: Standard dry fly, sizes 16 to 8.
THREAD: 8/0 or 6/0 in a color to match the body.
WINGS: Elk hair.
TAIL: Elk hair.
BODY: Dubbing.
HACKLE: Two hackles, one wound parachute style around each wing.

COMMENTS: The Waterwalker can be tied in a variety of colors. It is sort of a double parachute—clever.

ROYAL HUMPY   WHITE WULFF   BRAIDED BUTT DAMSEL

CLARK'S DAMSELFLY   CLUMPER MIDGE   MADAM X

MUDDLER (Dry)   RENEGADE   WATERWALKER